WILLIAM CAREY
AND THE MISSIONARY VISION

WILLIAM CAREY
AND THE MISSIONARY VISION

DANIEL WEBBER

THE BANNER OF TRUTH TRUST

THE BANNER OF TRUTH TRUST
3 Murrayfield Road, Edinburgh EH12 6EL, UK
P.O. Box 621, Carlisle, PA 17013, USA

ISBN 0 85151 921 0

Typeset in 11/14 pt Sabon at
the Banner of Truth Trust
Printed in the U.S.A. by
Versa Press, Inc.,
East Peoria, IL

TO MY COLLEAGUES AT THE
EUROPEAN MISSIONARY FELLOWSHIP
WHOSE SYMPATHY WITH WILLIAM CAREY'S
VISION IS EVIDENT IN ALL THEIR LABOURS

Contents

Preface

The primary purpose of this slim volume is to tell the heroic story of William Carey's passionate advocacy of world mission. It is of course understandable that when the story of a life like his is recounted, most of the attention should focus on what he actually achieved in India two hundred years ago. However, what is less well-known is the earlier story of how, almost single-handedly, he did what no other person in the English-speaking world had done before him. As a dedicated and determined servant of God, William Carey is rightly credited with putting world mission at the heart of the church's concern for a fallen world. It is for this that he is often referred to as 'the father of modern missions'. This particular part of his story is intimately bound up with the writing of the *Enquiry* (to give it its abbreviated title), in which Carey sets out the *raison d'être* for his most persuasive missionary apologetic.

Foremost among the reasons for retelling this story is the simple fact that the single most urgent need of the world is to hear the gospel of the grace of God in Jesus Christ. There are, of course, a great many needs in a fallen world. All have the right to hope that 'men and women of good will' shall do all that they can to alleviate the appalling suffering and anguish which constantly threaten to overwhelm the lives of so many. Christian people, of course, will also play their part in this vital work. Nevertheless, the church's primary task remains what it has always been: to 'go into all the world and preach the gospel to every creature'. And yet our concern is that the church is in very real danger of losing sight of the primacy of this particular responsibility. The world is a contagious place, and in a climate in which media and celebrity attention count for so much, too often the church seems mesmerized by the world's agenda. The example of William Carey – who was far from being unconcerned about the world's general plight – may yet have the power both to clarify our vision and arouse our compassion in favour of the ultimate needs of mankind. It is with this hope in mind that the contents of this book have been compiled.

The work itself is very much a joint effort. Its contents span four centuries and contain three parts. The first section is entirely my own work and therefore I must bear responsibility for it. *William Carey and the Missionary Vision* represents a version of an address I first gave at the Carey Ministers' Conference in Swanwick in 1992. This was the occasion of the two-hundredth anniversary of the first publication of Carey's *Enquiry*. In summary form it seeks to tell the story of Carey's passionate concern for the evangelization of the world. The limited purpose of the lecture was to highlight this remarkable man's dogged determination to stir the consciences of eighteenth-century Christian men and women in favour of involvement in overseas mission. In my opinion, a similar and urgent appeal is now in need of being taken to a new generation of evangelical believers.

A form of my original address was first published in 1993. To my surprise, it quickly sold out. Several times since then I have been asked if I intended to have the lecture republished. But even though it is now little more than a decade on since that original publication, I doubted whether anyone would be sufficiently interested in repeating the exercise. I had not, however, counted on the enthusiasm of Jonathan Watson, the General Editor at the Banner of Truth Trust. He was present at Swanwick when that original address was given, and it is largely due to his interest in its content that a fully revised edition now appears in this new format.

The second part of this work is from the pen of William Carey himself. It is a reprint of *An Enquiry into the Obligations of Christians to Use Means for the Conversion of the Heathens*. Hailed by no less a person than Professor J. Herbert Kane (1910–88) as 'a landmark in Christian history' which 'deserves a place alongside Martin Luther's Ninety-five Theses', the *Enquiry* is still capable of stirring hearts and minds more than two hundred years after its first appearance.

Originally printed in 1792, what we have included here is an almost exact copy of a facsimile edition which was republished in 1961. I have made some changes to the original text, but these are minimal. I have added biblical references where Carey's quotations had none. The section including Carey's 'Survey of the Present State of the World' contains all the original material and will be of great interest to those who wish to gain some insight into the extent of Carey's amazing research. Many of the place names Carey listed in the tables of his 'Survey' have changed over the 213 years since this document was first published, but I have not altered their original form.

The final piece, and shorter than the other two, is a sermon preached by Andrew Fuller. It is called, *The Instances, the Evil Nature, and the Dangerous Tendency of Delay, in the Concerns of Religion*. One of Carey's most able supporters, Fuller preached this sermon to a gathering of the Northamptonshire and Leicestershire ministers at Clipstone on 27 April 1791. To read this sermon now is still a very moving experience and, in some ways, it proved a turning point in the realization of Carey's vision. Just one month later, Carey's *Enquiry* was published.

Although there was still much to be done before the establishment in the following year of the Particular Baptist Society for the Propagation of the Gospel to the Heathen, from this moment onwards the impetus that would take Carey to his eventual triumphs in India was unstoppable.

In commending these works I wish to acknowledge my indebtedness to a number of people who have made it possible. In addition to Jonathan Watson, whom I have already mentioned, I am again indebted to Joan McWilliams for her patience in reading through this material and sorting out my own feeble efforts at trying to reproduce Carey's tables. I am also deeply grateful for the patient and continuing support of my wife, Zurilia. I am dedicating this book to members and friends associated with the European Missionary Fellowship, with whom I have now had the privilege of working for more than fifteen years.

DANIEL WEBBER
Welwyn, Hertfordshire
July 2005

PART 1

WILLIAM CAREY AND THE MISSIONARY VISION

Daniel Webber

I

Introduction

William Carey is often referred to as 'the father of modern missions', but not because he was the first. He was not even the first Protestant missionary; neither was his the first missionary endeavour of significance. More than a century earlier, John Eliot (1604–90) had conducted effective evangelistic work among the Algonquin Indians of North America, and there had also been some notable work done by German Pietists supported by the Danish-Halle Mission. Indeed, by the time Carey had set sail, the Moravians had already completed valuable work in India.

He is given this title because he was largely responsible for turning the tide of Protestant thought in favour of foreign missions. Ruth Tucker, in her work on the history of missions, *From Jerusalem to Irian Jaya*, says of Carey that 'More than any other individual in modern history, he stirred the imagination of the Christian world and showed by his own humble example what could and should be done to bring a lost world to Christ.'[1] Similarly, Stephen Neill, in his *A History of Christian Missions*, speaks of Carey's work as representing a turning point. He says that, 'It marks the entry of the English-speaking world on a large scale into the missionary enterprise.'[2]

In order properly to understand this, certain background details need to be borne in mind. First, for all its spiritual power and vitality, the Reformation had had little time to devote to missions. For some time it still represented a small and fragile minority with battles to fight on many fronts. Second, the eighteenth century was 'the age of reason', the age of the Enlightenment. Many of its clergymen believed that the Great Commission was only given to the apostles, that its work had been fulfilled in previous ages, and that it is therefore to be assumed that the heathen world had rejected the gospel and must now await its fate on the Day of Judgment. Moreover, for some, any form of enthusiasm was simply anathema. It should be remembered that even as late as 1796 the General Assembly of the Church of Scotland – albeit not without protest – passed by a majority the motion that 'to spread abroad the knowledge of the gospel among the barbarous and heathen nations seems to be highly preposterous'.[3] As we shall have occasion to observe, the brand of Calvinism advocated by some Particular Baptists of the time was very often little better in its missionary outlook.

Fortunately, there was a third and highly significant influence on the life of eighteenth-century Britain, which made Carey's vision for the evangelization of the world not only a possibility, but a reality. The Great Awakening, which was largely associated with the preaching of George Whitefield (1714–70) and John Wesley (1703–91), had swept through the English-speaking world in the earlier part of the century. Nevertheless, the predominant view with respect to mission was still the one described above. Essentially, it was not viewed as part of the church's current or continuing responsibility.

The story of how William Carey fundamentally altered that outlook is to be the main subject of this brief investigation. We shall not, except incidentally, be examining his theology, which was of the best Calvinistic sort. Neither is it our intention to concentrate on biography, except in so far as it sets the scene for our main interest. It is our intention to focus attention on what was originally and unpretentiously referred to as a pamphlet written by Carey and first published over two hundred years ago in 1792. Although not a best-seller at the time, Carey's faith in its content went on to contribute to the formation of the Particular Baptist Missionary Society in the same year and much of the missionary endeavour of the following century. It is the story of the birth and implement-ation of the concern of this remarkable statement that we shall consider. And, having done so, we shall seek to draw lessons from its content, convinced that Carey's concerns should be of vital interest to the church of this day. Some believe that his work is still the most convincing missionary appeal ever written. J. Herbert Kane goes as far as to assert that 'Carey's *Enquiry* was . . . a landmark in Christian history and deserves a place alongside Martin Luther's *Ninety-five Theses* in its influence on subsequent church history.'[4] It certainly expresses a mighty vision; one that is as needy today as it has ever been. Twenty-first-century Christians certainly need to recapture his vision.

NOTES:

[1] Tucker R., *From Jerusalem to Irian Jaya* (Grand Rapids: Zondervan, 1983), p. 114.

[2] Neill S., *A History of Christian Missions* (London: Hodder and Stoughton, 1978), p. 26.

[3] Quoted from Walker F. D., *William Carey: Missionary Pioneer and Statesman* (London: SCM, 1926), p. 100.

[4] Kane J. H., *A Concise History of the Christian World Mission* (Grand Rapids: Baker Book House, 1982), p. 85.

2

The Preparation of the Man

Before we can consider Carey's missionary vision, we must give some general consideration to the man. Particularly, we must consider the preparation of the man. It is God's normal way to take people where they are, and with what they are, to make them the servants they are subsequently to be. In grace he moulds and matures the character of his people through their particular circumstances.

With the advantage of living more than two centuries after the publication of his *Enquiry*, and with the heroic story of his missionary labours completed, it is easy to recognize in the early Carey signs of the man he was to become. But if we had been present at his birth, or only witnessed the circumstances of his upbringing, how different our outlook and expectation might have been. Why, even his own father thought him mad when in his early thirties William announced that he was to be a missionary in India.

1. *FROM BIRTH TO REBIRTH*
Born in the village of Paulerspury, some ten miles south of Northampton in 1761, William Carey's upbringing was hard. In addition, he had little formal education and was largely self-taught. And yet, the persistence for which he was later known was evident in measure even in those formative years. His brother, Thomas, was later to make the following observation concerning his character:

7

> I . . . recollect that he was, from a boy . . . always resolutely
> determined never to give up any point or particle of any thing
> on which his mind was set, till he had arrived at a clear
> knowledge and sense of his subject. He was neither diverted
> from his object by allurements, nor driven from the search of it
> by threats or ridicule . . . [5]

He was interested in all forms of life: plants and flowers, birds and insects. Species both alive and dead filled his bedroom. As a youth he took great delight in his father's garden and here no doubt acquired some of the patience and learned to absorb the disappointment inevitably involved in such interests. The lesson that there are few worthwhile quick returns in life was to prove a valuable one.

For all its hardships, however, his home life seems to have been a happy one. He was the eldest of five and his father became the village schoolmaster and parish clerk. One of the great advantages that this brought the young Carey was access to books, which he read assiduously. Strangely enough, in view of the climate for which he was destined, a skin disease made it too painful for him to be exposed to the sun's full glare and necessitated that an indoor trade be found for him. Northampton being an important centre for shoemaking, he was apprenticed to a Clarke Nichols in Piddington. Apart from the trade that was subsequently to enable him to earn something of a living, this move was to have two additional benefits. The first was to find himself working alongside another apprentice three years his senior. Unlike Carey, John Warr was a Dissenter. Having only known attendance at an Anglican Church, Carey was later to offer the following observations on his own contributions to the lively discussions that ensued in the shoemaking shop.

> I had a share of pride sufficient for a thousand times my
> knowledge . . . I also made up in positive assertion what was
> wanting in argument, and generally came off with triumph. [6]

Despite this boast, Warr's testimony clearly had an effect on him. Not only did the position of the Dissenters seem more reasonable than he had previously supposed, but his own conduct also gave him cause for concern about his eternal position. The incident that seemed most to have affected him in this respect took place during the period leading up to Christmas time. It was the custom in those days for apprentices to receive Christmas gifts from their master's customers. As Carey was collecting his he was surprised by the question of an ironmonger who asked if he would prefer to receive a shilling or a sixpence. Without hesitation, he chose the shilling. Later, however, having already decided on a number of articles he wished to buy, Carey was dismayed to discover that he had been deceived. The shilling he had been given was a counterfeit.

He decided to remedy the situation by exchanging the counterfeit coin for a shilling he had collected on his master's behalf. In a letter later written to Andrew Fuller (1754–1815) he speaks of this episode, and of the way in which he had sought to appease his nagging conscience.

> I . . . therefore came to the resolution to declare strenuously that the bad money was his [his master's]. I well remember the struggles of mind which I had on this occasion, and that I made this deliberate sin a matter of prayer to God as I passed over the fields home. I there promised, that if God would but get me clearly over this, or, in other words, help me through with the theft, I would certainly for the future leave off all evil practices; but this theft and consequent lying appeared to me so necessary, that they could not be dispensed with. A gracious God did not get me safe through.[7]

As that final sentence indicates, God was 'gracious' and refused to participate in his intended deception. Mr Nichols sent another apprentice to the trader in order to be reimbursed and, of course, Carey's guilt was established. Such was the young man's shame and remorse that for some time he would neither go out nor attend any place of worship.

Once he did venture outdoors, he began attending prayer meetings more regularly. Although still nominally a member of the Anglican Church, on 10 February 1779, he made the decision to cease attending what he described as 'a lifeless, carnal ministry' in preference for one that was 'more evangelical'. The occasion was a Sunday that had been set apart by King George III as a national day of prayer and fasting on account of the war that was going badly against the American colonies. Along with John Warr, Carey found himself listening to a powerful sermon at the Meeting House in Hackleton. The sermon, based on Hebrews 13:13, called for a complete commitment to Christ and it seems to have spoken directly to Carey. He came away from the meeting convinced that he should leave the Church of England and identify himself with the Dissenters where he 'would find guidance along the way of the cross'.[8]

2. EARLY GROWTH AND RESPONSIBILITIES

Another far-reaching consequence of Carey's apprenticeship was that his master allowed him access to his books. This, in turn, led him to seek out a certain Tom Jones – a university drop-out – in order to gain an understanding of New Testament Greek. When, in 1779, Nichols died, Carey's apprenticeship was transferred to a relative of his former master, Mr Thomas Old of Hackleton. He used to receive visits from Thomas Scott of Olney (1747–1821) who made the following remark about Carey: 'I from the first thought young Carey an extraordinary person.'[9]

Still not quite twenty years old, William Carey married his master's sister-in-law, Dorothy Plackett on 10 June 1781. She was nearly six years older than he and her father was leader of the Hackleton Meeting. There is no good reason to suspect that in these early years, at least, theirs was anything other than a happy marriage. Indeed, even later on, when Dorothy's mental condition was so poor and the relationship under strain, Carey seems to have been a most considerate husband. Their first sorrow, however, came with the death of their first-born child. Ann died of a fever which troubled the entire family and almost proved fatal to Carey himself.

Despite such difficulties and great sorrows, Carey continued his studies and preached regularly. His views were still maturing but, among other books, he readily testified to the help he received from Robert Hall's *Help to Zion's Travellers*. At about the same time his thoughts began to turn to believers' baptism and on 5 October 1783 he was eventually baptized in the River Nene at Northampton by John Ryland, Jr. (1753–1825).

On 31 December 1783, Thomas Old died and Carey took over both the business and the responsibility of caring for his master's widow and four children. There could hardly have been a more inopportune time to do so. Trade was particularly bad after Britain's humiliating defeat in America. Moreover, the winter of 1783–84 was one of the coldest on record. Then, on top of it all, Carey was seriously cheated by one of his customers.

NOTES:

[5] Quoted from Drewery M., *William Carey* (London: Hodder and Stoughton, 1978), p. 25.

[6] Dakin A., *William Carey: Shoemaker, Linguist, Missionary* (London: The Carey Press, n.d.), p. 12.

[7] Quoted from Drewery, op. cit., p. 16.

[8] ibid., p. 19.

[9] ibid., p. 20.

3

The Missionary Vision

Throughout his years at Piddington, though under-nourished and constantly struggling against persistent coughs and fever, Carey endeavoured to scrape a living for the needs of seven people. Then, in 1785, an opportunity arose for him to move to Moulton to be the preacher to a small Baptist community there. The church had been without a minister for ten years, services had become infrequent and the building had fallen into disrepair. His stipend was £10 per annum, supplemented by £5 from a London fund. He was no better off than he had been before, but initially, at least, he was able to supplement his income through teaching.

1. THE BIRTH OF HIS MISSIONARY VISION

The origin of his interest in missions also began around this time, as he himself was later to disclose. He wrote: 'My attention was first awakened after I was at Moulton, by reading the *Last Voyage of Captain Cook.*'[10] Actually, his interest in Cook had first been aroused whilst still a schoolboy and he had followed the accounts of Cook's voyages as they were published in the *Northampton Mercury*. However, in his new state of heart and mind this book became a revelation of human need. These 'savages' were now seen as God's creatures and in need of a Sovereign's mercies.

From that time he began reading and collecting all the information that he could find about the peoples of those lands that knew nothing of the love of God in Jesus Christ. A large home-made map of the world was fixed to the schoolroom wall and on it he kept records of all the information that he had gathered from his studies.

The church to which he was ministering prospered, but the school did not. Alas, the children deserted him and he had to return to shoemaking in order to supplement his income. Although a preacher at Moulton, he became a member of the Baptist Church in Olney on 14 July 1785. The pastor at Olney was John Sutcliff (1752–1814). Carey intimated that he wished to enter the ministry but, after hearing him preach, the members decided he needed a period of probation before ordination. This finally came on Wednesday, 1 August 1787. In addition to Sutcliff, John Ryland, Jr. and Andrew Fuller officiated.

He continued to devour every book on missions that he could find. He read what he could of the exploits of pioneer missionaries, making careful notes on everything as he went along. A particularly important influence on his life at this time was Andrew Fuller's *The Gospel Worthy of All Acceptation*. Published in 1784, on its title page stood the great missionary text: 'Go ye into all the world and preach the gospel to every creature.' As a result of reading this work, it became immediately clear to him that if it was the duty of all men to believe the gospel, then it was equally the duty of those who had been entrusted with the gospel to endeavour to make it known to all nations. But this was still the eighteenth century. Prejudice, even within his own evangelical circles, was largely against such an enterprise. What was he to do? This was just as clear: he must seek to arouse men and women to the need for mission, and the place to start was with the church's ministers.

In 1786 Carey was present at a ministers' meeting in Northampton. Towards evening, when the public services were over and some were sitting in discussion, Mr Ryland Sr. invited one of the younger men to propose a subject for discussion.

Carey suggested the following motion:

> Whether the command given to the apostles to teach all nations was not obligatory on all succeeding ministers to the end of the world, seeing that the accompanying promise was of equal extent.

The reply from the older man came like a thunderbolt:

> Young man, sit down: when God pleases to convert the heathen, he will do it without your aid or mine.[11]

At least, this was how the matter was later reported by Mr Morris, minister of Clipstone, who was present at the meeting. This incident serves to provide some idea of the immense difficulties facing Carey even within his own constituency. The hyper-Calvinism of the day was more than capable of turning the sovereignty of God into a pretext for doing nothing.

2. *A PASSIONATE ADVOCATE OF WORLD MISSION*

Discouraged, but not dissuaded, Carey embarked upon the task of educating all with whom he came into contact about the great need for missions. He preached about it to his little flock and echoes of the same concern were to be found in his public prayers. At several ministers' meetings between 1787 and 1790 this was his chief topic of conversation. Some of the older men in particular thought his was a wild and impracticable scheme, but he continued undaunted. Mary Drewery informs us that Carey

> set down on paper a detailed analysis of the state of the world as he saw it, the need for missionary enterprise and the methods by which it should be carried out. In addition, he took in turn each of the arguments advanced against missionary endeavour and proceeded to demolish it.[12]

This proved to be the first draft of the *Enquiry*. In it, the map on his wall became a weapon; its details became arrows.

George Smith says of it:

The *Enquiry* has a literary interest of its own, as a contribution to the statistics and geography of the world, written in a cultured and almost finished style, such as few, if any, University men of that day could have produced, for none were impelled by such a motive as Carey had. In an obscure village, toiling save when he slept, and finding rest on Sunday only by a change of toil, far from the libraries and the society of men with more advantages than his own, this shoemaker, still under thirty, surveys the whole world, continent by continent, island by island, race by race, faith by faith, kingdom by kingdom, tabulating his results with an accuracy, and following them up with a logical power of generalization, which would extort the admiration of the learned men even of the present day.[13]

But we shall come to its content later.

While on a tour in Birmingham collecting funds for his little chapel at Moulton, he met a Mr Thomas Potts. A wealthy man, Potts promised to put up £10 towards the publication of the *Enquiry*. On his return he called in on John Ryland, Jr. in Northampton; Fuller and Sutcliff were also present. They knew nothing of the pamphlet he had already written. He earnestly sought them to write a book on the subject and in the warmth of his enthusiasm confessed that Mr Potts had promised £10 if he would publish such a work. They urged him to write, but not to be in too much of a hurry to publish. When, in a short while, he produced it for their examination and correction, they found little to alter, but still advised delay.

At approximately the same time, 'a wave of prayer was sweeping over the Baptist churches of the Midlands'.[14] Some ministers had been influenced by the writings of Jonathan Edwards. As a result of reading his *An Humble Attempt to Promote Explicit Agreement and Visible Union of God's People in Extraordinary Prayer for the Revival of Religion and the Advancement of Christ's Kingdom on Earth*, a resolution

had been formed at the annual meeting of the Ministers' Association at Nottingham in 1784, to establish regular meetings to
pray for 'the revival of our churches and the spread of the
gospel'. Such meetings were actually being held in many of the
churches of the Northamptonshire and Leicestershire
Association on the first Monday evening in every calendar
month and from 1786 the Midland Baptist Association
followed their example; then Yorkshire adopted the practice
too.

In February 1789 Carey received a call from Harvey Lane
Chapel, Leicester. Many trials awaited him there, but 'firmness
and tact, patience and faith, triumphed'.[15] Radical 'surgery'
was employed and blessing followed. If anything, his workload
increased. An idea of Carey's regular activity is inadvertently
recorded for us in a letter written by him to his father and
dated 12 November 1790. It reads:

> On Monday I confine myself to the study of the learned lang-
> uages, and oblige myself to translate something. On Tuesday to
> the study of science, history, composition, etc. On Wednesday I
> preach a lecture, and have been for more than twelve months on
> the Book of Revelation. On Thursday I visit my friends. Friday
> and Saturday are spent in preparing for the Lord's Day, and the
> Lord's Day in preaching the Word of God. Once a fortnight I
> preach three times at home; and once a fortnight I go to a
> neighbouring village in the evening. Once a month I go to
> another village on the Tuesday evening. My school begins at
> nine o'clock in the morning, and continues till four o'clock in
> winter and five in summer. I have acted for this twelve month as
> secretary to the committee of dissenters; and am now to be
> regularly appointed to that office, with a salary. Add to this
> occasional journeys, ministers' meetings, etc., and you will
> rather wonder that I have any time, than that I have so little.

There then follows this most telling comment, one which
explains so much of Carey's outlook: 'I am not my own, nor

would I choose for myself. Let God employ me where He thinks fit.'[16]

And yet, despite pastoral problems, domestic difficulties, and a telling workload, his burden for the evangelization of the world was not lessened. Fuller writes:

> The other ministers . . . had been compelled to think of the subject by his repeatedly advancing it, and they became desirous of it, if it could be accomplished; but feeling the difficulty of setting out in an unbeaten path, their minds revolted at the idea of attempting it. It seemed to them something too great, and too much like grasping at an object utterly beyond their reach.[17]

But this actually represented a considerable advance on the prejudice that had first greeted his concern in 1786. Now, at least, there was a company of men no longer opposed in principle to the notion. They just thought it impossible for the time being.

It was, in fact, Andrew Fuller who gave the decisive answer to this objection and fresh impetus to Carey's vision. On 27 April 1791 there was a meeting of the Northamptonshire and Leicestershire ministers at Clipstone at which Sutcliff and Fuller were the preachers. No doubt both sermons were intended to bring the issue to a head. Sutcliff spoke of the 'Zeal for the Lord of Hosts' and Fuller's text was Haggai 1:2: 'Thus speaketh the LORD of hosts, saying, This people say, The time is not come, the time that the LORD's house should be built.' The title of this sermon was, *The Instances, Evil Nature, and the Dangerous Tendency of Delay in the Concerns of Religion.* In his introduction Fuller points out that

> There is something of this procrastinating spirit running through a great part of life, and it is of great detriment to the work of God. We know of many things that should be done, and cannot in conscience directly oppose them; but still we find excuses for our inactivity . . . We quiet ourselves with the thought that they need not be done just now.

This plea . . . prevents us from undertaking any great or good work for the cause of Christ or the good of mankind . . . There are difficulties in the way, and we wait for their removal. We are very apt to indulge in a kind of prudent caution (as we call it) which foresees and magnifies difficulties beyond what they really are . . . It becomes us to beware lest we account that impossible which only requires such a degree of exertion as we are not inclined to give it . . . Perhaps the work requires expense . . . Perhaps it requires concurrence, and we wait for everybody to be of one mind, which is never to be expected . . . Instead of waiting for the removal of difficulties, we ought, in many cases to consider them as purposely laid in our way in order to try the sincerity of our religion.[18]

Later he goes on:

Let it be further considered whether it is not owing to this principle that so few, and so feeble efforts have been made for the propagation of the Gospel in the world . . . Are the souls of men of less value than heretofore? No. Is Christianity less true or less important than in former ages? This will not be pretended. Are there no opportunities . . . to convey the Gospel to the heathen? This cannot be pleaded so long as opportunities are found to trade with them, yea, and (what is a disgrace to the name of Christianity!) to buy them and sell them, and treat them with worse than savage barbarity. We have opportunities in abundance: the improvement of navigation and the maritime and commercial turn of this country furnish us with these; and it deserves to be considered whether this is not a circumstance that renders it a duty particularly binding on us. The truth is, we wait for we know not what: we seem to think 'the time is not come, the time for the spirit to be poured down from on high' . . . We pray for the conversion of the world and yet we neglect the ordinary means by which it can be brought about . . . How shall they hear without a preacher? And how shall they preach except they be sent?[19]

At the sermon's close, Carey at once urged that the ministers present resolve to form a missionary society. But still they hesitated. Several adjourned to the manse to discuss Carey's proposal.

They sat up late into the night; so late that they required a second supper! Eventually, and partly to humour their enthusiastic brother, they recommended a revision of his book and its printing 'for the consideration of the religious public'. Carey revised the manuscript.

3. THE CONTENT OF THE 'ENQUIRY'

On 24 May 1791, less than a month after Fuller's searching sermon at Clipstone, a company of ministers gathered at Carey's chapel in Leicester to ordain him officially to the pastorate upon which he had entered almost two years before. At their request that evening Carey read to Fuller, Ryland, Sutcliff, Samuel Pearce of Birmingham (1766–92) and Hopper (of Nottingham) a good deal of his revised manuscript. It won their approval and within a year it was published under the title, An Enquiry into the Obligations of Christians to Use Means for the Conversion of the Heathens, in which the religious state of the different nations of the world, the success of former undertakings, and the practicability of further undertakings, are considered. It is to the content of this small book that we shall now turn.

This remarkable document was unique in every way. It was, says Walker, 'a reasoned statement of Christian obligation, of world needs, of existing opportunities, and practical proposals for the formation of a Missionary Society.'[20] The reference to 'a reasoned statement' is important. It is exactly this. Although Carey had a great passion for the cause he advocated it was not, as we shall see, a case of all heart, no head. This was not only a matter of seeing a need and trying to meet it, but essentially one of obedience to God and to that which he had revealed in his Word.

A brief introduction explains the purpose and scope of the book. It begins irresistibly:

> As our blessed Lord has required us to pray that his kingdom may come and his will be done on earth as it is in heaven, it becomes us not only to express our desire of that event by words, but to use every lawful method to spread the knowledge of his name. In order to do this, it is necessary that we should become in some measure acquainted with the religious state of the world; and as this is an object we should be prompted to pursue not only by the gospel of the Redeemer, but even by the feelings of humanity . . . conscientious activity therein would form one of the strongest proofs that we are the subjects of grace.[21]

Here are Carey's missionary motives: love for and obedience to the God who had redeemed him, and the state of the world without Christ. It is because of this twofold consideration that the people of God are obliged 'to use every lawful method to spread the knowledge of his name'. He then succinctly outlines the scope of his work's concern.

> In order that the subject may be taken into more serious consideration, I shall enquire whether the commission given by our Lord to his disciples be not still binding on us – take a short view of former undertakings – give some account of the present state of the world – consider the practicability of doing something more than is done – and the duty of Christians in general in this matter.[22]

i. *The binding nature of the Great Commission*

His first section is headed, 'An Enquiry whether the Commission given by our Lord to His disciples be not still binding on us.' Here in a few short, sharp sentences, he answers the excuses that people were making in his day. His initial answer to those who suggest that 'if God intends the salvation of the heathen, he will some way or other bring them to the Gospel, or the Gospel to them' is really an excuse for the love of ease and the absence of compassion for the plight of lost sinners. Carey was supposed to have told the younger Ryland that this question was suggested by his father's famous rebuke at the Northampton meeting more than five years earlier.

As for the argument that the command 'to teach the nations' was only intended for the apostles, then presumably so too was the command to baptize and the promise, 'Lo, I am with you alway, even to the end of the world.' As for the difficulties, these had already been overcome by others. Roman Catholics had done so; and the Moravians were currently seeking to do so.

Moreover, traders were not being put off from seeking their gain by the difficulties involved. And, if it really was bad to preach to them [even in those days there were those in Britain who believed that upsetting the natives with religion was against their vested interests], then it must also be bad to pray for them. He even joins issue with those who speak about saving the 'home heathen' first!

ii. *A survey of missionary activity from Pentecost onwards*

Having argued that the commission given by our Lord to his original disciples was still binding on the church, he moves on in the second section to survey missionary effort from the time of Pentecost to his own day. Although he begins with the pioneer works carried on in England and Northern Europe, even the Portuguese Jesuits get a mention. The sheer volume of information that he brings together in this section is simply breathtaking.

When Carey turns to modern missions, he gives greater length to the works of John Eliot, David Brainerd, and others among the North American Indians. He then takes in the Danish and Dutch missions, before closing with two short paragraphs on the Moravians and John Wesley.

iii. *A survey of the world as a mission field*

In some ways the third section is the most remarkable of all. It is a careful survey of the whole world as then known. It contains twenty-three pages of statistical tables; a monument to his prodigious industry and indefatigable patience. Every table consists of five columns covering details such as the name of the country or island, its length and breadth, the number of inhabitants, and details of each nation's religion. His plodding is clearly in evidence. He covers even the tiniest islands. He then proceeds to analyse each in turn. This compilation is certainly not the result of guesswork. The whole section provides evidence of wide and painstaking research.

iv. *Facing the challenges of missionary endeavour*

The fourth section takes up the question of 'the practicability of something being done for the conversion of the heathen'. He recognizes the seriousness of some of the difficulties involved. He is very much aware of the fact that to many he and his concerns are simply those of a wild enthusiast. Nevertheless, not only does he provide cogent reasons for not allowing some of these difficulties to deter, but also he is not slow to draw attention to some of the truer motives residing in the hearts of many who were against the work.

The first difficulty envisaged is simply that of the great distances separating his countrymen from those he would have evangelized. He readily acknowledges that this would have been a problem but for the invention of the mariner's compass that now allows men to 'sail with as much certainty through the great South Sea as they can through the Mediterranean or any lesser sea'.[23] Moreover, he urges them to recognise the beckoning hand of Providence in the fact that commercial traders have been sent on ahead, blazing a trail before them. Ships had already been sent to explore places of recent discovery and parts unknown. And, he argues, 'every fresh account of their ignorance, or cruelty, should call forth our pity, and excite us to concur with providence in seeking their eternal good.'[24] Drawing on Isaiah 60:9, he argues that Scripture itself seems to point to this as a method by which God carries on his work. He sends the traders out in order that others with far better wares may follow.

The second difficulty has to do with the people to whom they were being exhorted to go and in particular 'their uncivilised and barbarous way of living'. This, he thought, was a poor argument for not going to them with the gospel. Indeed, according to Carey, this should be seen as a positive incentive to go. This excuse, he argues, can really only be an objection for those 'whose love of ease renders them unwilling to expose themselves to inconvenience for the good of others'.[25] Certainly, he goes on to say, such 'was no objection to the apostles and their successors, who went among the barbarous Germans and Gauls, and still more barbarous Britons!'[26] And what is more, it had not stopped traders, whose only interest was temporal profit. There is an understandable degree of sarcasm here from a man who had struggled with poverty and hunger in order to be of service to God. But there is an even greater reason for not being hindered by such things: compassion. It will also serve, as it had done among those to whom Eliot and Brainerd had ministered, to ennoble these very people. He writes:

> Can we as men, or as Christians, hear that a great part of our fellow-creatures, whose souls are as immortal as ours, and who are as capable as ourselves, of adorning the gospel, and contributing by their preaching, writings, or practices to the glory of our Redeemer's name and the good of his church, are enveloped in ignorance and barbarism? Can we hear that they are without the gospel, without government, without laws, and without arts, and sciences; and not exert ourselves to introduce among them the sentiments of men, and of Christians? Would not the spread of the gospel be the most effectual means of their

civilisation? Would not that make them useful members of society?[27]

The third difficulty was, of course, the very real possibility of being killed by the people to whom he was proposing they should go. It will be remembered that Captain Cook had himself been killed in 1779. Carey's response was that

> it is true that whoever does go must put his life in his hand, and not consult with flesh and blood; but do not the goodness of the cause, the duties incumbent on us as the creatures of God and Christians, and the perishing state of our fellow-men, loudly call upon us to venture all, and use every warrantable exertion for their benefit?[28]

And, in any case, the thought of being killed had not deterred the apostles. Had not Paul and Barnabas hazarded their lives for the sake of the gospel? Had not Eliot, Brainerd, and the Moravians done the very same thing? He also questioned whether the people to whom they were going were really as bad as they had been painted. Carey thought it just as likely that many of the barbarities reportedly suffered by those who had previously visited the so-called savages were acts of self-defence. Certainly many of the missionaries he had already mentioned had seldom been molested. Therefore, he seriously wondered whether the problems encountered or anticipated were not more the result of the local people coming into contact with the vices of nominal Christians.

The fourth difficulty was that of providing for the necessities of life. It was true, he replied that it may prove difficult to eat European food, but they could, after all, procure and subsist on that which satisfies the natives. One wonders if there isn't a touch of irony here. He certainly intends to challenge those who might be guilty of raising such objections. After all, what did they expect when they entered upon the high calling of the Christian ministry? Was it not inherent in their calling that it would involve self-denial? He writes:

A Christian minister is a person who in a peculiar sense is not his own; he is the servant of God, and therefore ought to be wholly devoted to him. By entering on that sacred office he solemnly undertakes to be always engaged, as much as possible, in the Lord's work, and not to choose his own pleasure, or employment, or pursue the ministry as a something that is to subserve his own ends, or interests, or as a kind of bye-work. He engages to go where God pleases, and to do or endure what he sees fit to command, or call him to, in the exercise of his function. He virtually bids farewell to friends, pleasures, and comforts, and stands in readiness to endure the greatest sufferings in the work of his Lord, and Master. It is inconsistent for ministers to please themselves with thoughts of a numerous auditory, cordial friends, a civilised country, legal protection, affluence, splendour, or even a competency. The slights, and hatred of men, and even pretended friends, gloomy prisons, and tortures, the society of barbarians of uncouth speech, miserable accommodations in wretched wildernesses, hunger, and thirst, nakedness, weariness, and painfulness, hard work, and but little worldly encouragement, should rather be the objects of their expectation.[29]

And with this still in mind, Carey seriously questions whether all ministers are justified in remaining in their country of origin when so many are perishing without means of grace in other lands. He continues:

Sure I am that it is entirely contrary to the spirit of the gospel for its ministers to enter upon it from interested motives, or with great expectations. On the contrary, the commission is a sufficient call to them to venture all, and, like the primitive Christians, go everywhere preaching the gospel.[30]

When we remember his poverty, it is easy to see how this could not be regarded as too serious a problem. Nevertheless, he does provide this further practical suggestion:

It might be necessary . . . for two, at least, to go together, and in general I should think it best that they should be married men, and to prevent their time from being employed in procuring necessaries, two or more other persons, with their wives and families, might also accompany them, who should be wholly employed in providing for them.[31]

He then goes on to outline his plans for a small community of men, accompanied by their wives and children, all working for the common good. They could cultivate a small plot of land as a resource when supplies failed and, of course, they would be company for each other. It is also more likely that they would become self-supporting far more quickly; an important issue as far as Carey was concerned. It was with this in mind that they should possess practical skills and the implements for carrying them out. Much of this strategy was to become a reality at Serampore.

The final difficulty was 'the unintelligibleness of their languages'. Remember that by this time the shoemaker/pastor had already mastered six languages (Latin, Greek, Hebrew, Italian, French, and Dutch)! His response to this was to suggest that in the early stages at least they should employ the same methods as do nations in similar circumstances seeking to engage in trade with each other: they should use interpreters. But missionaries are to be patient and mingle with the population with a view to learning the language as quickly as possible. In his view, this should not be too difficult to accomplish. He writes:

It is well known to require no very extraordinary talents to learn, in the space of a year, or two at most, the language of any people upon earth, so much of it at least as to be able to convey any sentiments we wish to their understandings.[32]

Carey then closes this section with one and a half pages on personal qualifications for missionary service. As this is so important to the matters we shall later return to later, it is appropriate that we should quote Carey even more fully. He writes:

> The Missionaries must be men of great piety, prudence, courage, and forbearance; of undoubted orthodoxy in their sentiments, and must enter with all their hearts into the spirit of their mission; they must be willing to leave all the comforts of life behind them, and to encounter all the hardships of a torrid or a frigid climate, an uncomfortable manner of living, and every other inconvenience that can attend this undertaking . . . They must be very careful not to resent injuries which may be offered to them, nor to think highly of themselves, so as to despise the poor heathens, and by those means lay a foundation for their resentment or rejection of the gospel. They must take every opportunity of doing them good, and labouring and travelling night and day, they must instruct, exhort, and rebuke, with all long suffering and anxious desire for them, and, above all, must be instant in prayer for the effusion of the Holy Spirit upon the people of their charge. Let but missionaries of the above description engage in the work, and we shall see that it is not impracticable.
>
> It might likewise be of importance, if God should bless their labours, for them to encourage any appearances of gifts amongst the people of their charge; if such should be raised up many advantages would be derived from their knowledge of the language and customs of their countrymen; and their change of conduct would give great weight to their ministrations.[33]

v. *The implementation of this missionary vision*

One might imagine that Carey would have been content to conclude at this point, but he is not quite finished. He knows that it is one thing to demonstrate the obligation and answer objections to its implementation, but it requires more if this vision is to become a reality. Therefore, the fifth and final section of this work goes on to make a practical application of his great theme. How is the work to be done? How is it to be set in place and carried on? Essentially his answer is twofold: it is to be accomplished through prayer and effort. First, there must be fervent, definite, and united prayer. This is how absolute dependence on God is properly expressed; and prayer to God is the only real hope for the success of any venture, especially this one. Carey had already learned a great deal in this respect in getting thus far; it was not to be forgotten now, nor in the years that lay ahead.

But prayer was not to stand alone. He writes: 'We must not be contented however with praying, without exerting ourselves in the use of means for the obtaining of those things we pray for.'[34] Once again he draws on the analogy of the trading company:

> When a trading company have obtained their charter they usually go to its utmost limits; and their stocks, their ships, their officers, and men are so chosen and regulated as to be likely to answer their purpose; but they do not stop here, for encouraged by the prospects of success, they use every effort, cast their bread upon the waters, cultivate friendship with every one from whose information they expect the least advantage. They cross the widest seas and encounter the most unfavourable climates . . . and sometimes undergo the most affecting hardships . . . Christians are a body whose truest interest lies in the exaltation of the Messiah's Kingdom. Their charter is very extensive, their encouragements exceedingly great . . . Let then every one in his station consider himself as bound to act with all his might, and in every possible way for God.[35]

But how? The first step was to establish a missionary society that would have responsibility for planning and directing the work, collecting funds and sending forth the missionaries. He proposed that the Particular Baptists should proceed to form a society of their own and make a start. His choice of this body of believers was not suggested by any narrowness of outlook, but rather because he recognized the reality of things as they were. He says that 'in the present divided state of Christendom, it would be more likely for good to be done by each denomination engaging separately in the work . . . There is room enough for us all.'[36]

Even though he wanted works established to be self-supporting as quickly as possible he knew, in view of the vastness of the task and the immediate needs, that money would have to be raised. He proposed that this should be done by rich Christians devoting a portion of their wealth to the work and that people in moderate circumstances should give a tenth of their income to it. Those who were poor should contribute 'one penny or more per week according to their circumstances'.[37] Ever with a social conscience, he was aware that some Christians were protesting against the slave trade by not using sugar which was being obtained through this means. This, he estimated, was saving some families between sixpence and a shilling each week. Why not devote such savings to missionary work? Then comes the final appeal: 'Whatsover a man soweth that shall he also reap.'

> What a treasure, what an harvest must await such characters as Paul, and Eliot, and Brainerd . . . What a heaven will it be to see the many myriads of poor heathens, of Britons among the rest, who by their labours have been brought to the knowledge of God. Surely a crown of rejoicing like this is worth aspiring to. Surely it is worth while to lay ourselves out with all our might in promoting the cause and kingdom of Christ.[38]

And with this he finishes. Well, not quite.

4. THE FORMATION OF THE MISSIONARY SOCIETY

The publication of the *Enquiry* was, of course, but a means to an end. Unless he could press home its message, and secure the formation of the society it advocated, all would still be lost. And so, in the spring of 1792 there was a meeting of the Baptist Ministers' Association at Nottingham and Carey was the appointed preacher. In the Baptist Chapel in Park Street, Nottingham, he announced his text as Isaiah 54:2–3: 'Enlarge the place of thy tent, and let them stretch forth the curtains of thine habitations: spare not, lengthen thy cords, and strengthen thy stakes; for thou shalt break forth on thy right hand and on the left; and thy seed shall inherit the Gentiles, and make the desolate cities to be inhabited.'

After a brief introduction, Carey took up what he regarded as the spirit of the passage in two memorable exhortations: 'Expect great things from God. Attempt great things for God.' This sermon drew from the younger Ryland the following comment:

> It was as if the sluices of his soul were thrown fully open and the flood that had been accumulating for years rushed forth in full volume and irresistible power . . . If all the people had lifted up their voices and wept . . . I should not have wondered at the effect, it would have only seemed proportionate to the cause; so clearly did he prove the criminality of our supineness in the cause of God.[39]

The following morning the ministers met alone for their usual conference and Carey's proposal that they form a society came up for discussion. However, the enthusiasm of the day before had already passed and, once again, the practical difficulties seemed everything. They felt that the whole venture was simply beyond their ability. They again concluded that the proposal was impossible. In distress, Carey seized Fuller's arm and, with obvious emotion, enquired whether they were to part once again without doing anything definite. A sudden change came over the whole meeting. After further discussion, and passionate pleading from Carey, it was decided to place in their minutes the following resolution:

> [That] a plan be prepared against the next ministers' meeting for forming a Baptist Society for propagating the gospel among the heathens.[40]

On 2 October 1792, the autumn meeting of the Association was held in Fuller's chapel in Kettering, Northamptonshire. In the evening, twelve ministers, a student, and a layman met to discuss the missionary scheme. Still they wavered. It was not that they were unsympathetic to Carey's vision, but most still felt that the time was not right. A long series of wars, culminating in the loss of the American colonies, had impoverished the country. France had descended into anarchy and even England was in a state of restlessness. The project itself would cost a great deal of money, they only represented the Particular Baptists in Northamptonshire, Bedfordshire, Leicestershire, and Nottinghamshire, and their congregations were mainly made up of peasants. But, as this small gathering hovered on the brink of hesitation, Carey made another opportune appeal. He pulled from his pocket a little volume entitled, *Periodical Account of Moravian Missions,* and, pointing to it, declared, 'If only you had read this and knew how these men overcame all obstacles for Christ's sake, you would go forward in faith!'[41] The effect was immediate and overwhelming. The Minute Book for that day contains the following resolutions:

1. Desirous of making an effort for the propagation of the gospel among the heathen, agreeably to what is recommended in brother Carey's late publication on that subject, we, whose names appear to the subsequent subscription, do solemnly agree to act in society together for that purpose.

2. As in the present divided state of Christendom it seems that each denomination, by exerting itself separately, is most likely to accomplish the great ends of a mission, it is agreed that this society be called The Particular Baptist Society for Propagating the Gospel among the Heathen.

3. As such an undertaking must needs be attended with expense, we agree immediately to open a subscription for the above purpose, and to recommend it to others. [There then follows a

list containing the names of twelve ministers and one layman and the initial sum contributed to the enterprise. John Ryland and Reynold Hogg lead the way with two guineas; five others and Mr Joseph Timms donate one guinea; and the rest subscribe ten shillings and sixpence. A total of £3.12s.6d].

4. Every person who shall subscribe ten pounds at once or ten shillings and sixpence annually, shall be considered a member of the society.

5. That the Revs. John Ryland, Reynold Hogg, William Carey, John Sutcliff, and Andrew Fuller be appointed a Committee, three of whom shall be empowered to act in carrying into effect the purposes of this society.

6. That the Rev. Reynold Hogg be appointed treasurer, and the Rev. Andrew Fuller, secretary.

7. That the subscriptions be paid in at the Northampton ministers' meeting, October 31st, 1792, at which time the subject shall be considered more particularly by the Committee, and other subscribers who may be present.[42]

No money was actually collected at the meeting just described. Instead, promises were collected on slips of paper and placed in Andrew Fuller's tobacco box. Incidentally, this box had a relief picture of the conversion of Paul, the missionary to the Gentiles, on its lid! Some might think that appropriate! One of the interesting features of the subscribers' list is the absence of Carey's name on it. It may simply have been that he was too poor to do so. Alternatively, it is to be remembered that he had already donated the proceeds from his book. Whatever the reason, he was soon to 'give himself away'.

5. TURNING RESOLUTIONS INTO ACTION
We are nearly at the end of the main part of our story. Nevertheless, as everyone who has ever been involved in such

meetings and passed resolutions knows, such activities alone do not get anything done. The great feature of the resolution was that it was a resolution to act. As we know, William Carey was at the forefront of this action too. Up until this point his task had been to convince ministers of their obligation and bring them to a determination to act. The first step was to raise sufficient money to enable the enterprise to proceed. The great difference now, of course, was that he had colleagues who were willing to throw themselves unsparingly into it. Ryland, Fuller, Sutcliff, Pearce, and Carey were to meet to discuss ways and means.

Carey and Fuller were not present at the first appointed meeting, but donations were already to hand totalling £88. 18s.od. At the second such gathering, also held in Northampton, they considered matters of policy. Questions were discussed on the qualifications for missionaries, those who were known and thought to be qualified, the regulations to be adopted concerning them, and the parts of the world to which they should immediately turn their attention. It was soon after this that John Thomas was brought to their attention. He had already been to India as a doctor with the Royal Navy and stayed on to minister as a free-lance doctor and evangelist. He became the new society's first missionary. When a volunteer was sought as 'a suitable companion', not surprisingly, it was William Carey who volunteered.

At first, his church was unwilling to lose him. His father thought him mad. Even his wife was determined not to accompany him. Yet such was Carey's commitment that he was prepared to go even without her! The rights and wrongs of this have been debated ever since. What no one can deny is that here was a man prepared and suited to the task. He had already been an inspiration to others and was now willing to give himself without hesitation, and wholeheartedly, to a work to which he was persuaded God had called him.

NOTES:

[10] Quoted from Walker, op. cit., p. 56.

[11] Marshman J. C., *The Story of Carey, Marshman & Ward* (London: Alexander Strathan, 1864), p. 11.

[12] ibid., p.31.

[13] Smith G. A., *The Life of William Carey D.D.: Shoemaker and Missionary* (London: John Murray, 1885), pp. 32–33.

[14] Walker, op. cit., p. 67.

[15] ibid., p. 73.

[16] ibid., pp. 72–73.

[17] ibid., p. 74.

[18] Fuller A., *Complete Works* (London: Henry G. Bohn, 1853), pp. 550-551.

[19] ibid., p. 551.

[20] Walker, op. cit., p. 79.

[21] *An Enquiry into the Obligations of Christians to Use Every Means for the Conversion of the Heathens* (1792), New facsimile edition 1961, (Oxford: Baptist Missionary Society, 1991), p. 31.

[22] ibid., p. 33.

[23] ibid., p. 93.

[24] ibid., pp. 93–94.

[25] ibid., p. 94.

[26] ibid., p. 94.

[27] ibid., pp. 95–96.

[28] ibid., p. 96.

[29] ibid., pp. 97–98.

[30] ibid., pp. 98–99.

[31] ibid., p. 99.

[32] ibid., p. 100.

[33] ibid., p. 100–102.

[34] ibid., p. 107.

[35] ibid., pp. 107–108.

[36] ibid., p. 109.

[37] ibid., p. 111.

[38] ibid., p. 112.

[39] Walker, op. cit., p. 94.

[40] ibid., pp. 94–95.

[41] ibid., p. 97.

[42] ibid., p. 98-99.

4

The Vision in Practice

In many ways the next part of William Carey's story is the most exciting and challenging aspect of his life and vision. It is not, however, the main focus of this particular investigation. We have deliberately chosen to limit our attention to those events which contributed to the initial implementation of his missionary vision. Nevertheless, something ought to be said about the way in which Carey sought to put his theories into practice.

Even before he and John Thomas could set sail for India, there were two obstacles to overcome. The first involved their immediate need of funds. Together with John Thomas, Carey embarked on a hectic speaking and fund-raising tour for the new mission. This turned out to be more demanding than originally anticipated. John Thomas had incurred a considerable number of debts, and his creditors were demanding payment. Quite apart from the problem itself, the effect of this was to delay their originally intended sailing date. The second and the much more difficult issue as far as Carey was concerned, was his wife's unwillingness to accompany him. Even though he himself was still determined to go, Dorothy's persistent refusal to go with him deeply grieved Carey. In the end, it was their enforced delay, and the persuasive powers of John Thomas, that proved decisive in bringing about the required change of mind. There was, however, to be one final condition; Dorothy's sister, Katherine Plackett, was to be allowed to accompany them. This was agreed and the party finally set sail from Dover on 13 June 1793.

A five-month journey through violent storms eventually concluded with their arrival in India on 19 November 1793. Theirs was not, however, a warm welcome. Missionaries were generally unwelcome in India. And those, like this group, who had arrived without first securing the appropriate licence, were even less welcome than others.

1. *EARLY YEARS IN INDIA*

As a consequence, the early years in India were very difficult. Even the immediate start was somewhat inauspicious and not only because they had arrived without visas. They had some difficulty finding accommodation; at least, the Careys did. John Thomas was able to secure accommodation in Calcutta itself; eventually the Careys had to settle for a malaria-infested marsh outside the city. Housing, food, and healthcare were hopelessly inadequate. As a consequence, just one year after their arrival, five-year-old Peter succumbed to dysentery. This proved to be a trauma that Dorothy was unable to endure. Sadly, her already unstable mental condition deteriorated. She was later described by a missionary as 'wholly deranged' and eventually died in 1807.

These years must have taxed even the staying power of Carey to the absolute limit. After seven years of struggle, including language study, itinerant preaching, and secular employment in an indigo factory, Carey was unable to claim one Indian convert. Yet in many other respects this was a most fruitful period. He had used the time to acquire a remarkable grasp of the language, translated a large portion of the New Testament into Bengali, planted a tiny non-Indian church in Malda, and had made the name of Christ known throughout much of Northern Bengal. But these small beginnings were soon to give way to something far better with the crucial move at the end of the nineteenth century to Serampore. In this

Danish colony he was also out of reach of the troublesome East India Company.

2. SERAMPORE

The move to Serampore in 1800 was largely precipitated by the arrival of the first new party of missionaries from England. It was a decisive move that multiplied opportunities for the struggling Baptist Missionary Society. Serampore was a more densely populated area than North Bengal and within a year Carey and his colleagues were able to report the conversion of two Indian nationals. By 1803 there were 25 baptized converts. Still the work was slow. Nevertheless, by 1818 some 600 had been baptized and several thousand were regularly attending classes and services.

One of the most important developments with this move was the emphasis that Carey gave to translating the Scriptures. The missionary base at Serampore became something of a linguistic centre. With the help of Indian teachers, a truly amazing quantity of work was undertaken. He completed six translations of the entire Bible (Bengali, Sanskrit, Oriya, Hindi, Assamese, and Marathi) and portions of the New Testament into nearly 30 additional languages. Another priority of this period was the establishment of an indigenous church. This was very much tied up with his translation work as he was convinced that the availability of the Scriptures would pave the way for a strong and indigenous church. Allied to this was a great emphasis on the training of nationals. Indeed, the first convert, Krishna Pal, was to serve as an effective evangelist in Calcutta and Assam.

In many ways Carey was far ahead of his time. This can be seen particularly in his emphasis on both the training of nationals, and his use of women. The task of evangelizing India was enormous and Carey quickly recognized that women would be needed if they were to reach Indian women, who were generally secluded from the outside world and beyond the reach of male missionaries. But then again, it is quite evident that he was prepared to use anyone in this great task. As a teacher in Fort William College he would even employ his non-Christian colleagues and students in translation work. Even his sons were not spared. At thirteen he set Jabez learning Chinese in order to help with translation. Felix was preaching at sixteen and his teenage son, William, was distributing literature. Other missionary children were also normally active in the cause.

Although a supporter of that which was good and useful in Indian culture, unlike some in today's missionary movement Carey was not unwilling to criticize, and even condemn, those aspects of the culture which he believed offended God. For example, he protested loudly against infanticide, child pros-titution, and sati (widow burning). In doing so he aided Hindu reformers who were able to influence legislation banning these practices. Carey, of course, had his critics. Many did not agree with his willingness to translate Eastern literature. There were also those who were unhappy about his willingness to allow non-Christians into Serampore College, which had been established essentially for the training of indigenous church-planters and evangelists in 1819.

Another important part of his outlook concerned his belief that missionaries should be as economically self-supporting as soon as possible. During his early years in India he had worked as a factory foreman. Later, he was a well-paid language professor at Fort William College in Calcutta. In addition, the Serampore mission was supported by funds from its boarding school. The mission itself operated on a communitarian basis, which allowed for funds not needed for living expenses to be used for the expansion of mission work. The important thing to remember about all this, however, is that all these activities were subservient to, and pursued in, the interests of the greater work of making the gospel known as far and wide as possible.

Even that which we have so briefly outlined draws attention to the fact that that which was done in India between 1793 and

1834 was not the work of Carey alone. Indeed, without the able and harmonious assistance of Joshua Marshman and William Ward nothing like that which was accomplished could have been achieved. Together they were the backbone of the mission. He spoke warmly of their hard work and harmony. Sadly, this harmony was to be shattered when, after 15 years at Serampore, young missionaries arriving from England baulked at the practice of communitarianism and the authoritarian control exercised by the senior missionaries. The result was a temporary split that deeply grieved the self-sacrificing and peace-loving Carey.

Under God, of course, much of Carey's success was related to his personality and character. He once boasted that he could 'plod' and this was ably demonstrated when a warehouse fire destroyed not only valuable paper and equipment, but also irreplaceable manuscripts. Had he been made of different stuff, he may never have recovered. Instead, he accepted this as the will of God and immediately began the arduous task of redoing some of the translations that had been lost. Interestingly, news of the fire made Carey a household name in England. Not only were large sums of money sent from well-wishers of every evangelical denomination, but there was even a request for a portrait of the missionary. This caused Fuller to pen the following warning to Carey:

> The fire has given your undertaking a celebrity which nothing else, it seems, could; a celebrity which makes me tremble. The public is now giving us their praises. Eight hundred guineas have been offered for Dr Carey's likeness! If we inhale this incense, will not God withhold his blessing, and then where are we? Ought we not to tremble? Surely, all need more grace to go through good report than through evil . . . When the people ascribed 'ten thousands to David', it wrought envy in Saul, and proved a source of long and sore affliction. If some new trials were to follow, I should not be surprised; but, if we be kept humble and near to God, we have nothing to fear.[43]

This proved a timely warning, for many of Carey's most difficult times were still to come. We have neither the time nor space to record them here, but this letter itself gives some insight into the spirit that prevailed both with Carey and his friend, Andrew Fuller. In Fuller, Carey had a faithful and able apologist for the mission. But when in 1815 he died, then the difficulties that had simmered for some time concerning the relationship between the work in Serampore and the home Committee came to a head. It was to lead in 1826 to a temporary separation. Although this tie was later re-established, that, and the long years given to India, had detrimentally left their mark on Carey's health.

He continued to work, however, to within two years of his eventual death. From July 1833, with his health evidently declining, he suffered a series of strokes which left him temporarily paralysed. Through all this his third wife, Grace, devotedly cared for him. Even during this time he took great delight in his garden. Too weak to do much himself, he still enjoyed being wheeled around it. The following June he died peacefully and was buried at Serampore alongside the tomb of his much-loved second wife, Charlotte. At his request, a simple tablet marked his grave bearing the words:

> WILLIAM CAREY
> Born August 17th, 1761
> Died June 9th, 1834
>
> A wretched, poor, and helpless worm,
> On Thy kind arms I fall.

NOTE:
43 Quoted from Drewery, op. cit., p. 161.

5

The Challenge of Carey's *Enquiry*

In concluding this investigation, we must briefly return to the *Enquiry* once more. It was, as we have said, an amazing work. The zeal with which its vision was pursued by Carey both in gaining its acceptance and implementing its policies is something that ought still to call forth our admiration. A study of his life would appear to reveal that that which he had written in 1792 was essentially the pattern he followed in his labours, especially at Serampore. If there were differences between the written document and the practice they were almost all simply a matter of emphasis, experience adding fresh insight to the principles already set out. But one of the most remarkable things about the work is that, when it came to practice, there was little need for Carey to change what he had previously written.

Of course, this was largely due to his conviction that the principles themselves were biblical. Therefore, there was no need to be feverishly looking for a fresh gimmick, one that would change everything and bring in success. He was committed to that which he understood to be right, and content to leave the consequences with God. He was, after all, God's servant. And when things seemed to go against him, he was more willing to suspect himself than his methodology.

Now, from this man – his concern and method – we can still learn (or re-learn) a great deal today. We cannot possibly draw attention to all that we might, but it would be a dereliction of duty not to draw attention to certain basic concerns as expressed in Carey's small work, which we would do well to heed in our day.

1. THE OBLIGATION

It may hardly seem necessary for us to draw attention to the most fundamental concern of Carey's *Enquiry*, that of obligation. After all, this is not the eighteenth century, and we have had more than two hundred years of missionary endeavour since his day, and much good has already been done. Moreover, the work itself continues with much still being done that has both its origin and support from these shores. Nevertheless, our current position may not be quite as comfortable as we would like to imagine.

For example, if the funding of mission work is any sort of barometer by which to judge interest among the churches, then we may be in more trouble than we have hitherto thought. It is certainly true that a good number of missionary agencies based in the United Kingdom are finding it extremely difficult to support their *current activities*, let alone to give serious attention to the idea of expansion. Moreover, it is increasingly evident that attendance at missionary meetings is no longer what it used to be. These factors may in turn be related to others: there are those, for example, who would argue that most of our current difficulties relating to mission are the consequence of a general decline in Evangelicalism (or, at least, Evangelicalism of the traditional sort) in this country. Not without warrant, others would contend that there are now so many 'heathen' on our own doorsteps that our primary attention should be directed towards them. Then again there are those who give the impression that it may be more appropriate to postpone going to other shores until we have the revival that will guarantee our labour's success.

The trouble with most of these arguments is that they sound very much like the kind of things Carey was hearing in his day.

At times it must have seemed to him that he was the only one interested in the evangelization of the lost nations of the world. Yet the indifference of others around him did not stop Carey from seeking to rouse the apathetic, nor hinder him from being prepared to go himself. It is also true that the need at home is very great. Nevertheless, just to cite one example, in comparison with the rest of the continent of Europe, we are still very rich. We may be trading off the last throes of our historical legacy, but we are still under an obligation and we know of no better way of improving our own situation than by being faithful to all the obligations (at home and overseas) that God has cast into our lap.

We know that there may yet be other reasons why missionary agencies are somewhat out in the cold these days. There may simply be too many of them. It may be that there has been, in some cases, a breakdown in trust between churches and agencies. It could well be that some reformation is long overdue concerning the relationship between churches and agencies. It may even be that there is some doubt about whether there exists a biblical basis or rationale for mission agencies at all. All these are legitimate areas for discussion and Carey has much to teach us in these areas too. Nevertheless, none of these considerations ought to have the effect of lessening or undermining our sense of obligation to 'go into all the world and preach the gospel'. And, as Carey recognized, it is the ministers of the churches that have a particular responsibility to make these needs known to those under their charge; ever to keep before the minds and hearts of their hearers the urgent need of those who have never heard the gospel.

2. THE WORK ITSELF

A second area of challenge for some of us has to do with the nature of the work itself. To suggest that interest and support of missionary work in this country is in decline is really only part of the story. The fact is that large sums of money still leave these shores every year in the name of missionary endeavour, which for some of us is not, strictly speaking, *missionary work* at all. Increasing numbers of people are still leaving these shores to take up what by now is almost unquestioned missionary activity, but it is not to preach the gospel. It is not even primarily to preach the gospel. It is to serve – in hospitals and schools, in social and political arenas. And, by comparison, there is hardly any shortage of funds for such activities.

Perhaps part of the problem here rests with the term 'missionary' itself. Not being a biblical word, perhaps it is inevitable that it should now be put to use in a way that was not originally envisaged. Traditionally, at least in evangelical circles, it was a word normally associated with the activities of our Lord's early disciples as they attempted to begin the work of going 'into all the world to preach the gospel'. Today it is used to cover just about anything that is done by Christians in any country other than their own. This, we are persuaded, is at best regrettable; at worst it is mischievous. How so? Because the almost inevitable tendency of this outlook is for the preaching of the gospel to end up taking second place to humanitarian concern. It does so in terms of manpower; it does so in terms of funding; and it does so in terms of church interest and participation.

It is not that we are against the good being done by Christians all over the world. We praise God for it and them. It is not that we do not recognize in them faithful servants of God doing his will and to his glory. It is not that we are opposed to Christians who are missionaries in the traditional sense dirtying their hands in the very real problems faced by needy men and women in the third, or any other, world. It is that we are convinced that the work of the church is essentially something else. It is almost as an aside, by accident, that she finds herself involved in these other matters. She is commissioned to fulfil another work; a work that no one else is either interested in, or qualified to perform: the preaching of the gospel to needy sinners that they might be properly prepared for an everlasting state. It is a question of priority. It may even be a question of mandate. This is what she is uniquely called upon to do and all else must be subservient to it.

Now we know that William Carey was interested and involved in many things. He was not an obscurantist. He was not unconcerned about the social, educational, and environmental needs of those to whom he ministered. But we are persuaded that all these interests and concerns were subservient to this greater work of proclaiming the gospel. Stephen Neill, for example [additional comments have been placed within brackets], summarizes Carey's work as

> a five-pronged advance, with equal attention directed to each of the five elements: (1) the widespread preaching of the Gospel by every possible [Carey would have been more inclined to used the word 'lawful'] method; (2) the support of the preaching by the distribution of the Bible in the languages of the country [and where the Bible is in place we would probably advocate the use of good Christian literature]; (3) the establishment at the earliest possible moment of a Church; (4) a profound study of the background and thought of the non-Christian peoples; (5) the training at the earliest possible moment of an indigenous ministry [by our day we would want this to be a priority].[44]

This is the vision of missionary work that we need to recapture as a matter of the utmost urgency.

3. THE KIND OF PEOPLE THE WORK REQUIRES

Finally, if we are to encourage the sending of missionaries to other lands, and if we are to encourage nationals to aspire to this work, what kind of people ought they to be? The first answer to give is that they are to be the best. This work Carey believed was quite simply the highest to which any person could aspire. Indeed, when in 1814 his son, Felix, resigned from his missionary labours in order to become ambassador in Calcutta for the King of Burma, Carey wrote home lamenting that 'Felix is *shrivelled* [emphasis added] from a missionary into an ambassador.'[45] We wonder how many twenty-first-century Christian parents would see things in the same light?

What is needed is not simply a greater number of people willing to do the work, but more whose hearts, minds, and lives are in tune with the example set by William Carey. But how are we to recognize such people? Let us remind ourselves again of the yardstick set out in a few lines of the *Enquiry*:

> The missionaries must be men of great piety, prudence, courage and forbearance; of undoubted orthodoxy in their sentiments, and must enter with all their hearts into the spirit of their mission; they must be willing to leave all the comforts of life behind them, and to encounter all the hardships of a torrid or a frigid climate, an uncomfortable manner of living, and every other inconvenience that can attend this undertaking.[46]

In other words, they are to be people known for their Christian character and convictions, and who possess a willingness to give themselves wholeheartedly to a life of self-denial. It ought also to be said that these characteristics should, in meaningful measure, be evident in those who aspire to such work before they leave the land of their birth. Such qualities are not suddenly discovered once the aeroplane has touched down on some distant runway and the work is expected to begin. Carey himself was largely the man that he was because he had been well-prepared by life and grace before leaving for India. Furthermore, his was not merely a desire to preach, but a concern to reach lost and dying souls. Again, the evidence of his undoubted commitment to the eternal welfare of those living and dying without Christ can be seen long before he was physically among them. It is particularly evident in the way that, as a young man, he collected every possible detail that he

could about the circumstances of those he longed to reach; and
in the way in which he spread the details of these concerns
before the Lord in prayer, and before Christian gatherings on
every possible occasion.

There was also in his character a firm commitment to what
a former generation would have described as his *duty*, some
thing we fear that is largely lost on a generation that has
probably had things far too comfortable for its own good, and
the good of others. For Carey, however, this commitment to
duty meant that when the going got incredibly tough, and the
disappointments and sorrows were multiplying, there was no
talk of giving up. His sense of obligation to the task in hand
held him. He believed in hard work and expected that the way
would be difficult. And yet even this outlook was borne of a
genuine realism, rather than a pessimistic or depressive
disposition. The only success he sought was that he should be
faithful to God and the work entrusted to him; the only failure
that he shunned was that of not doing what needed to be done.
Indeed, much of his own attitude is revealed in a letter written
to another son in 1808. William Jr. was but twenty years old,
newly-wed, and posted to a remote area well-known for its
gangs of violent robbers and wild animals. He had been gored
by a buffalo and wrote to his father asking for permission to
return to Serampore. Among other things, his father's reply
contained the following admonition:

> I ought, however, to say that I think there is much guilt in your
> fears. You and Mary will be a thousand times more safe in
> committing yourselves to God in the way of duty than in
> neglecting obvious duty to take care of yourselves.[47]

His own commitment to duty and his great confidence in
God were, of course, rooted in his conviction that God was
sovereign over all things. This was not only so when things
seemed to run in his favour, but when providence seemed
against him. This is nowhere seen more clearly than in his

response to the devastating fire to which we have already referred, and which undid so much of his work; some of it irreplaceable. In a letter to Dr Ryland he states:

> The Lord has smitten us, he had a right to do so, and we deserve his corrections. I wish to submit to His sovereign will, nay cordially to acquiesce therein, and to examine myself rigidly to see what in me has contributed to this evil.[48]

This same attitude is evident again when as a sixty-two-year-old he found himself offering the following advice to a young missionary just commencing his labours:

> Remember three things. First, that it is your duty to preach the Gospel to every creature; second, remember that God has declared that His word shall accomplish that for which it is sent; third, that He can as easily remove the present seemingly formidable obstacles as we can move the smallest particles of dust.[49]

This is the kind of Christian that is needed in every walk of life, but particularly so on the mission field.

NOTES:
[44] Neill, op. cit., p. 263.
[45] Quoted from Drewery, op. cit., p. 166.
[46] Carey's *Enquiry*, op. cit., p. 100.
47 Quoted from Drewery, op. cit., p. 149.
48 ibid., p. 155.
49 Quoted from Dakin, op. cit., p. 77.

BIBLIOGRAPHY

Beck J. R., *Dorothy Carey*, Grand Rapids: Baker Book House, 1992.

Carey S. P., *William Carey D.D., Fellow of the Linnaean Society*, London: Hodder and Stoughton, 1923.

Carey W., *An Enquiry into the Obligations of Christians to Use Every Means for the Conversion of the Heathens* [1792], New facsimile edition with an Introduction by E. A. Payne (1961), Oxford: Baptist Missionary Society, 1991.

Dakin A., *William Carey: Shoemaker, Linguist, Missionary*, London: Carey Press, n.d.

Davis W. B., *William Carey: Father of Modern Missions*, Chicago: Moody Press, 1963.

Drewery M., *William Carey*, London: Hodder and Stoughton, 1978.

Finnie K. M., *William Carey: By Trade a Cobbler*, Eastbourne: Kingsway, 1986.

Fuller A., *The Complete Works*, London: Henry G. Bohn, 1853.

Fuller T. E., *A Memoir of the Life and Writings of Andrew Fuller*, London: J. Heaton & Son, 1863.

Gardner J., Ministering Men, or Heroes of Missionary Enterprise, London: James Blackwood, n.d.

George T., *Faithful Witness: The Life and Mission of William Carey*, Leicester: Inter-Varsity Press, 1991.

Haykin M. A. G., *One Heart and One Soul: John Sutcliff of Olney, His Friends and Times*, Darlington: Evangelical Press, 1994.

Kane J. H., *A Concise History of the Christian World Mission*, Grand Rapids: Baker Book House, 1982.

Latourette K. S., *A History of Christianity, Vol. 2* [Revised edition], New York: Harper & Row, 1975.

—— *A History of the Expansion of Christianity, Vols. 4 & 6*, Exeter: Paternoster Press, 1971.

Marshman J. C., *The Story of Carey, Marshman & Ward* [Popular Edition], London: Alexander Strathan, 1864.

Myers J. B. (ed.), *The Centenary Volume of the Baptist Missionary Society: 1792–1892*, London: Baptist Missionary Society, 1892.

Neill S., *A History of Christian Missions*, London: Hodder and Stoughton, 1965.

Payne E. A., *The First Generation*, London: Carey Press, 1936.

Smith G. A., *The Life of William Carey D.D., Shoemaker and Missionary*, London: John Murray, 1885.

Tucker R. A., *From Jerusalem to Irian Jaya*, Grand Rapids: Zondervan, 1983.

William Carey: Father of Modern Missions [in *Great Leaders of the Christian Church*, ed. J. D. Woodbridge], Chicago: Moody Press, 1988.

Walker F. D., *William Carey: Missionary Pioneer and Statesman*, London: SCM, 1926.

PART 2

AN ENQUIRY INTO THE OBLIGATIONS OF CHRISTIANS TO USE MEANS FOR THE CONVERSION OF THE HEATHENS

William Carey

1792

INTRODUCTION

As our blessed Lord has required us to pray that his kingdom may come, and his will be done on earth as it is in heaven, it becomes us not only to express our desire of that event by words, but to use every lawful method to spread the knowledge of his name. In order to do this, it is necessary that we should become in some measure acquainted with the religious state of the world; and as this is an object we should be prompted to pursue, not only by the gospel of our Redeemer, but even by the feelings of humanity, so an inclination to conscientious activity therein would form one of the strongest proofs that we are the subjects of grace, and partakers of that spirit of universal benevolence and genuine philanthropy which appear so eminent in the character of God himself.

Sin was introduced amongst the children of men by the fall of Adam, and has ever since been spreading its baneful influence. By changing its appearances to suit the circumstances of the times, it has grown up in ten thousand forms, and constantly counteracted the will and designs of God. One would have supposed that the remembrance of the deluge would have been transmitted from father to son, and have perpetually deterred mankind from transgressing the will of their Maker; but so blinded were they, that in the time of Abraham, gross wickedness prevailed wherever colonies were planted, and the iniquity of the Amorites was great, though not yet full. After this, idolatry spread more and more, till the seven devoted nations were cut off with the most signal marks of divine displeasure. Still, however, the progress of evil was not stopped, but the Israelites themselves too often joined with the rest of mankind against the God of Israel. In one period the grossest ignorance and barbarism prevailed in the world; and afterwards, in a more enlightened age, the most daring infidelity, and contempt of God; so that the world which was once over-run with ignorance, now 'by wisdom knew not God, but changed the glory of the incorruptible God' as much as in the most barbarous ages, 'into an image made like to corruptible man, and to birds, and four-footed beasts, and creeping things' (*1 Cor.* 1:21; *Rom.* 1:23). Nay, as they increased in science and politeness, they ran into more abundant and extravagant idolatries.

Yet God repeatedly made known his intention to prevail finally over all the power of the Devil, and to destroy all his works, and set up his own kingdom and interest among men, and extend it as universally as Satan had extended his. It was for this purpose that the Messiah came and died, that God might be just, and the justifier of all that should believe in him. When he had laid down his life, and taken it up again, he sent forth his disciples to preach the good tidings to every creature, and to endeavour by all possible methods to bring over a lost world to God. They went forth according to their divine commission, and wonderful success attended their labours; the civilized Greeks, and uncivilized barbarians, each yielded to the cross of Christ, and embraced it as the only way of salvation. Since the apostolic age many other attempts to spread the gospel have been made, which have been considerably successful, notwithstanding which a very considerable part of mankind is still involved in all the darkness of heathenism. Some attempts are still being made, but they are inconsiderable in comparison of what might be done if the whole body of Christians entered heartily into the spirit of the divine command on this subject. Some think little about it, others are unacquainted with the state of the world, and others love their wealth better than the souls of their fellow-creatures.

In order that the subject may be taken into more serious consideration, I shall (1) enquire, whether the commission given by our Lord to his disciples be not still binding on us, (2) take a short view of former undertakings, (3) give some account of the present state of the world, (4) consider the practicability of doing something more than is done, and (5) the duty of Christians in general in this matter.

SECTION ONE

AN ENQUIRY WHETHER THE COMMISSION GIVEN BY OUR LORD TO HIS DISCIPLES BE NOT STILL BINDING ON US

Our Lord Jesus Christ, a little before his departure, commissioned his apostles to 'Go' and 'teach all nations' (*Matt.* 28:19); or, as another evangelist expresses it, 'Go into all the world, and preach the gospel to every creature' (*Mark* 16:15). This commission was as extensive as possible, and laid them under obligation to disperse themselves into every country of the habitable globe, and preach to all the inhabitants, without exception, or limitation. They accordingly went forth in obedience to the command, and the power of God evidently wrought with them. Many attempts of the same kind have been made since their day, and which have been attended with various success; but the work has not been taken up, or prosecuted of late years (except by a few individuals) with that zeal and perseverance with which the primitive Christians went about it. It seems as if many thought the commission was sufficiently put in execution by what the apostles and others have done; that we have enough to do to attend to the salvation of our own countrymen; and that, if God intends the salvation of the heathen, he will some way or other bring them to the gospel, or the gospel to them. It is thus that multitudes sit at ease, and give themselves no concern about the far greater part of their fellow-sinners, who to this day, are lost in ignorance and idolatry. There seems also to be an opinion existing in the minds of some, that because the apostles were extraordinary officers and have no proper successors, and because many things which were right for them to do would be utterly unwarrantable for us, therefore it may not be immediately binding on us to execute the commission, though it was so upon them. To the consideration of such persons I would offer the following observations.

First, if the command of Christ to teach all nations be restricted to the apostles, or those under the immediate inspiration of the Holy Ghost, then that of baptizing should be so too; and every denomination of Christians, except the Quakers, do wrong in baptizing with water at all.

Secondly, if the command of Christ to teach all nations be confined to the apostles, then all such ordinary ministers who have endeavoured to carry the gospel to the heathens, have acted without a warrant, and run before they were sent. Yea, and though God has promised the most glorious things to the heathen world by sending his gospel to them, yet whoever goes first, or indeed at all, with that message, unless he have a new and special commission from heaven, must go without any authority for so doing.

Thirdly, if the command of Christ to teach all nations extend only to the apostles, then, doubtless, the promise of the divine presence in this world must be so limited; but this is worded in such a manner as expressly precludes such an idea. 'Lo, I am with you always, to the end of the world' (*Matt.* 28:20).

That there are cases in which even a divine command may cease to be binding is admitted. As for instance, if it be *repealed,* as the ceremonial commandments of the Jewish law; or if there be *no subjects* in the world for the commanded act to be exercised upon, as in the law of septennial release, which might be dispensed with when there should be no poor in the land to have their debts forgiven (*Deut.* 15:4); or if, in any particular instance, we can produce a *counter-revelation,* of equal authority with the original command, as when Paul and Silas were forbidden of the Holy Ghost to preach the word in Bythinia (*Acts* 16:6,7); or if, in any case, there would be a *natural impossibility* of putting it in execution. It was not the duty of Paul to preach Christ to the inhabitants of Otaheite, because no such place was then discovered, nor had he any means of coming at them. But none of these things can be alleged by us in behalf of the neglect of the commission given by Christ. We cannot say that it is repealed, like the commands of the ceremonial law; nor can we plead that there are no objects for the command to be exercised upon. Alas! the far greater part of the world, as we shall see presently, is still covered with heathen darkness! Nor can we produce a counter-revelation, concerning any particular nation, like that to Paul and Silas, concerning Bythinia; and, if we could, it would not warrant our sitting still and neglecting all the other parts of the world; for Paul and Silas, when forbidden to preach to those heathens, went elsewhere, and preached to others. Neither can we allege a natural impossibility in the case. It has been said that we ought not to force our way, but to wait for the openings, and leadings of providence; but it might with equal propriety be answered in this case, neither ought we to neglect embracing those openings in providence which daily present themselves to us. What openings of providence do we wait for? We can neither expect to be transported into the heathen world without ordinary means, nor to be endowed with the gift of tongues, etc., when we arrive there. These would not be providential interpositions, but miraculous ones. Where a command exists nothing can be necessary to render it binding but a removal of those obstacles which render obedience impossible, and these are removed already. Natural imposs-ibility can never be pleaded so long as facts exist to prove the contrary. Have not the popish missionaries surmounted all those difficulties which we have generally thought to be insuperable? Have not the missionaries of the *Unitas Fratrum*, or Moravian Brethren, encountered the scorching heat of Abyssinia, and the frozen climes of Greenland, and Labrador, their difficult languages, and savage manners? Or have not English traders, for the sake of gain, surmounted all those things which have generally been counted insurmountable obstacles in the way of preaching the gospel? Witness the trade to Persia, the East Indies, China, and Greenland, yea even the accursed Slave-Trade on the coasts of Africa. Men can insinuate themselves into the favour of the most barbarous clans, and uncultivated tribes, for the sake of gain; and however different the circumstances of trading and preaching are, yet this will prove the possibility of ministers being introduced there; and if this is but thought a sufficient reason to make the experiment, my point is gained.

It has been said that some learned divines have proved from Scripture that the time is not yet come that the heathen should be converted; and that first *the witnesses must be slain* (*Rev.* 11:1–13), and many other prophecies fulfilled. But admitting this to be the case (which I much doubt)[1] yet if any objection is made from this against preaching to them immediately, it must be founded on one of these things: either that the secret purpose of God is the rule of our duty, and then it must be as bad to pray for them, as to preach to them; or else that none shall be converted in the heathen world till the universal downpouring of the Spirit in the last days. But this objection comes too late; for the success of the gospel has been very considerable in many places already.

It has been objected that there are multitudes in our own nation, and within our immediate spheres of action, who are as ignorant as the South-Sea savages, and that therefore we have work enough at home, without going into other countries. That there are thousands in our own land as far from God as possible, I readily grant, and that this ought to excite us to tenfold diligence in our work, and in attempts to spread divine knowledge among them is a certain fact; but that it ought to supersede all attempts to spread the gospel in foreign parts seems to want proof. Our own countrymen have the means of grace, and may attend on the word preached if they choose it. They have the means of knowing the truth, and faithful ministers are placed in almost every part of the land, whose

[1] See *Edwards on Prayer*, on this subject, lately reprinted by Mr Sutcliffe.

spheres of action might be much extended if their congregations were but more hearty and active in the cause: but
with them the case is widely different, who have no Bible, no
written language (which many of them have not), no ministers,
no good civil government, nor any of those advantages which
we have. Pity, therefore, humanity, and much more Christianity, call loudly for every possible exertion to introduce the
gospel amongst them.

SECTION TWO

CONTAINING A SHORT REVIEW OF FORMER UNDERTAKINGS FOR THE CONVERSION OF THE HEATHEN

Before the coming of our Lord Jesus Christ the whole world
were either heathens, or Jews; and both, as to the body of
them, were enemies to the gospel. After the resurrection the
disciples continued in Jerusalem till Pentecost. Being daily
engaged in prayer and supplication, and having chosen
Matthias to supply the place of Judas in the apostolic office, on
that solemn day, when they were all assembled together, a most
remarkable effusion of the Holy Spirit took place, and a
capacity of speaking in all foreign languages was bestowed
upon them. This opportunity was embraced by Peter for
preaching the gospel to a great congregation of Jews and proselytes, who were from Parthia, Media, Elam, Mesopotamia,
Judea, Cappadocia, the proconsular Asia, Phrygia, Pamphylia,
Egypt, Lybia, Crete, Arabia, Rome, etc., and at the first effort
God wrought so powerfully that three thousand were
converted, who immediately after were baptized, and added to
the church. Before this great addition they consisted of but
about 'an hundred and twenty persons' (*Acts* 1:15), but from
that time they constantly increased (*Acts* 2). It was but a little
after this that Peter and John, going up to the temple, healed
the lame man; this miracle drew a great multitude together, and
Peter took occasion while they stood wondering at the event to
preach Jesus Christ to them (*Acts* 3).

The consequence was that five thousand more believed (*Acts* 4:4).

This was not done without opposition; the priests and Sadducees tried all the methods they could invent to prevent them from preaching the gospel. The apostles, however, asserted their divine warrant, and as soon as they were set at liberty addressed God, and prayed that a divine power might attend their labours, which petition was heard, and their future ministry was very successful. On account of the needs of those who were engaged in this good work, those amongst them who had possessions, or goods, sold them, and devoted the money to pious uses (*Acts* 4).

About this time a man and his wife, out of great pretence of piety, sold an estate, and brought part of the money to the apostles, pretending it to be the whole; for which dissimulation both he and his wife were struck dead by the hand of God. This awful catastrophe however was the occasion of many more men and women being added to the church. The miracles wrought by the apostles, and the success attending their ministry, stirred up greater envy in the priests and Sadducees, who imprisoned them; from which confinement they were soon liberated by an angel; upon which they went immediately as they were commanded and preached in the temple: here they were seized, and brought before the council, where Gamaliel spake in their favour, and they were dismissed. After this they continued to prosecute their work, rejoicing that they were counted worthy to suffer shame for the name of Christ (*Acts* 5).

By this time the church at Jerusalem was so increased that the multiplicity of its temporal concerns was the occasion of some neglects, which produced a dissatisfaction. The apostles, therefore, recommended to the church to choose seven pious men, whose office it should be to attend upon its temporal affairs; that 'they might give themselves to prayer, and the ministry of the word' (*Acts* 6:4). Seven were accordingly chosen, over whom the apostles prayed, and ordained them to the office of Deacons by imposition of hands: and, these things being settled, the church increased more and more (*Acts* 6). One of these Deacons, whose name was Stephen, being a person of eminent knowledge and holiness, wrought many miracles, and disputed with great evidence and energy for the truth of Christianity, which raised him up a number of opponents. These soon procured his death, and carried their resentment so far as to stir up such a persecution that the church, which till now had been confined to Jerusalem, was dispersed, and all the preachers except the apostles were driven thence, and went everywhere preaching the word (*Acts* 7:1–8:4).

A young man whose name was Saul was very active in this persecution; he had been educated under Gamaliel, a member of the Sanhedrin, was a person of promising genius, by profession a Pharisee, and much attached to the Jewish ceremonies. When Stephen was stoned he appeared much pleased with it, and had the custody of the clothes of his executioners; and from that time was fired with such a spirit of persecution himself, that he went about dragging some to prison, and compelling others to blaspheme the name of the Lord Jesus. Neither was he contented with exercising his rage at Jerusalem, but went to the chief priests and obtained testimonials of authority to carry on the same work at Damascus. But on his way, as he was almost ready to enter into the city, the Lord changed his heart in a very wonderful manner; so that instead of entering the town to persecute, he began to preach the gospel as soon as he was able. This presently brought upon him the same persecution which he had designed to exercise upon others, and even endangered his life, so that the brethren found it necessary to let him down the city wall in a basket by night, and so he escaped the hands of his enemies. From thence he went to Jerusalem where he preached the word, but being persecuted there he went to Cesarea, and from thence to Tarsus (*Acts* 9:1–30).

In the time of this trouble in the church, Philip went and preached at Samaria with great success, nay so great was the work that an impostor, who had deceived the people with legerdemain tricks for a long time, was so amazed, and even convinced, as to profess himself a Christian, and was baptized; but was afterwards detected, and appeared to be an hypocrite. Besides him a great number believed in reality, and being baptized a church was formed there. Soon after this the Lord commanded Philip to go the way which led from Jerusalem to Gaza, which he did, and there found a eunuch of great authority in the court of Ethiopia, to whom he preached Christ, who believed, and was baptized; after which Philip preached at Ashdod, or Azotus (*Acts* 8).

About the same time Peter went to Lydda, or Diospolis, and cured Eneas of a palsy, which was the means of conversion not only of the inhabitants of that town, but also of the neighbouring country, called Saron, the capital of which was Lasharon; and while he was there, a circumstance turned up which tended much to the spread of the truth. A woman of Joppa, a sea-port town in the neighbourhood, died and they sent to Lydda for Peter who went over, and when he had prayed she was raised to life again; which was an occasion of the conversion of many in that town. Peter continued preaching there for some time, and lodged at the house of a tanner (*Acts* 9:32–43).

Now another circumstance also tended to the further propagation of Christianity, for a Roman military officer who had some acquaintance with the Old Testament Scriptures, but was not circumcised, was one day engaged in prayer in his house at Cesarea, when an angel appeared to him, and bid him send for Peter from Joppa to preach in his house. Before this the work of God had been wholly confined to the Jews, and Jewish proselytes, and even the apostles appeared to have had very contracted ideas of the Christian dispensation; but now God by a vision revealed to Peter that Christianity was to be spread into all nations. He accordingly went and preached at the house of Cornelius, at Cesarea, when several were converted, and baptized, and the foundation of a church laid in that city (*Acts* 10).

Some of the dispersed ministers, having fled to Antioch in Syria, began to preach to the Greeks in that city about the same time, and had good success; upon which the apostles sent Paul and Barnabas, who instructed and strengthened them, and a church was formed in that city also, which in a little time sent out several eminent preachers (*Acts* 11:19–26).

In the Acts of the Apostles we have an account of four of the principal journeys which Paul and his companions undertook. The first, in which he was accompanied by Barnabas, is recorded in the thirteenth and fourteenth chapters, and was the first attack on the heathen world. It was a journey into Asia Minor. On their way they passed over the island of Cyprus. No sooner had they entered on their undertaking than they met with great difficulty; for Mark, whom they had taken as their minister, deserted them, and returned to Jerusalem, where, it seems, he thought he should enjoy the greatest quiet. Paul and Barnabas however went forward; in every city they preached the word of the Lord, entering into the Jewish synagogues and first preaching Christ to them, and then to the Gentiles. They were heard with great eagerness and candour by some, and rejected by others with obstinacy and wrath, and cruel persecution. On one occasion they had enough to do to restrain the people from worshipping them as gods, and soon after that Paul was stoned, dragged out of the city, and left for dead. Having penetrated as far as Derbe, they thought it proper to return by the way that they came, calling at every city where they had sown the good seed. They found in most, if not all these places, some who had embraced the gospel, and exhorted and strengthened them in the faith. They formed them into churches, and ordained them elders, and fasted and prayed with them; and so having commended them to the Lord on whom they had believed, returned to Antioch in Syria, from whence they first set out, and rehearsed to the church all that God had done with them, and how He had opened the door of faith to the Gentiles (*Acts* 13–14).

About this time a dispute arose in the churches concerning circumcision, and Paul and Barnabas were deputed to go up to Jerusalem, to consult the apostles and elders on the subject. The business being adjusted, they, accompanied with Judas and Silas, returned to Antioch with the general resolution, and continued there for a season, teaching and preaching the word of the Lord (*Acts* 15:1–35).

Paul now proposed to Barnabas, his fellow-labourer, that they might visit their brethren in the places where they had been already, and see how they did. To this Barnabas readily agreed, but a difference arising between them about taking with them John Mark, who had deserted them before, these two eminent servants of God were parted asunder, and never appear to have travelled together any more. They continued however each to serve in the cause of Christ, though they could not walk together. Barnabas took John, and sailed to Cyprus, his native island, and Paul took Silas, and went through Syria and Cilicia, to Derbe and Lystra, cities where he and Barnabas had preached in their first excursion (*Acts* 15:36–41).

Here they found Timothy, a promising young man, whom they encouraged to engage in the ministry.

Paul being now at Lystra, which was the boundary of his first excursion, and having visited the churches already planted, and delivered to them the decrees of the apostles and elders relating to circumcision, seems to have felt his heart enlarged, and attempted to carry on the glorious work of preaching the gospel to the heathen to a greater extent. With Silas and Timothy in his second journey[2] he took a western direction, passing through Phrygia, and the region of Galatia.

[2] The account of this second journey into the heathen world begins at Acts 15:40 and ends at chap. 18:22.

Having preached the word with considerable success,[3] he and his companions wished to have gone into the proconsular Asia, and afterwards tried to go into Bythinia; but being forbidden of the Holy Ghost, who seems to have had a special design of employing them elsewhere, passing by Mysia they came down to Troas on the sea-coast. Here a vision appeared to Paul, in which he was invited to go over to Macedonia. Obedient to the heavenly vision, and greatly encouraged by it, they with all speed crossed the Aegean Sea, and passing through the island of Samothracia, landed at Neapolis, and went from thence to Philippi, the chief city of that part of Macedonia. It was here that Paul preached on a Sabbath day to a few women by a river side, and Lydia, a woman of Thyatira, was converted and baptized, and her household with her. It was here that a poor girl, who brought her employers considerable profit by foretelling future events, followed the apostles, had her spirit of divination ejected, on which account her masters were much irritated, and raised a tumult, the effect of which was that Paul and Silas were imprisoned. But even this was over-ruled for the success of the gospel, in that the keeper of the prison, and all his house, were thereby brought to believe in the Lord Jesus Christ, and were baptized (*Acts* 16).

From Philippi they passed through Amphipolis, Apollonia, Thessalonica (now Salonichi), Berea, Athens, and Corinth, preaching the gospel wherever they went. From hence Paul took ship and sailed to Syria, only giving a short call at Ephesus, determining to be at Jerusalem at the feast of the Passover; and having saluted the church, he came to Cesarea, and from thence to Antioch (*Acts* 17:1–18:22).

Here ended Paul's second journey, which was very extensive, and took up some years of his time. He and his companions met with their difficulties in it, but had likewise their encouragements. They were persecuted at Philippi, as already noticed, and generally found the Jews to be their most

[3] See ch. 18:23 and *Gal.* 1:2.

inveterate enemies. These would raise tumults, inflame the minds of the Gentiles against them and follow them from place to place, doing them all the mischief in their power. This was the case especially at Thessalonica, Berea, and Corinth. But amidst all their persecutions God was with them, and strengthened them in various ways. At Berea they were candidly received, and their doctrine fairly tried by the Holy Scriptures; and 'therefore,' it is said, 'many of them believed' (*Acts* 17:12). At other places, though they affected to despise the apostle, yet some clave unto him. At Corinth opposition arose to a great height; but the Lord appeared to his servant in a vision, saying, 'Be not afraid, but speak, and hold not thy peace, for I am with thee, and no man shall set on thee to hurt thee; for I have much people in this city' (*Acts* 18:9, 10). And the promise was made abundantly good in the spirit displayed by Gallio, the proconsul, who turned a deaf ear to the accusations of the Jews, and nobly declined interfering in matters beside his province. Upon the whole a number of churches were planted during this journey, which for ages after shone as lights in the world.

When Paul had visited Antioch, and spent some time there, he prepared for a third journey into heathen countries, the account of which begins at *Acts* 18:23 and ends at *Acts* 21:17. At his first setting out he went over the whole country of Galatia and Phrygia in order, strengthening all the disciples; and passing through the upper coasts came to Ephesus. There for the space of three months he boldly preached in the Jewish synagogue, disputing, and persuading the things concerning the kingdom of God. But when the hardened Jews had openly rejected the gospel, and spake evil of that way before the multitude, Paul openly separated the disciples from them, and assembled in the school of one Tyrannus. This, it is said, continued for the space of two years, 'so that all who dwelt in' the proconsular 'Asia heard the word of the Lord Jesus, both Jews and Greeks' (*Acts* 19:10). Certain magicians about this time were exposed, and others were converted, who burnt their books and confessed their deeds. So mightily grew the word of the Lord, and prevailed.

After this, an uproar having been raised by Demetrius the silversmith, Paul went into Macedonia, visiting the churches planted in his former journey, and from thence passed into Greece. Having preached up and down for three months, he thought of sailing from thence directly to Syria; but in order to avoid the Jews, who laid wait for him near the sea coast, he took another course through Macedonia, and from thence to Troas, by the way of Philippi. There is no mention made in his former journey of his having preached at Troas; yet it seems he did, and a church was gathered, with whom the apostle at this time united in 'breaking of bread' (*Acts* 20:7). It was here that he preached all night and raised Eutychus, who being overcome with sleep had fallen down and was taken up dead. From thence they set sail for Syria, and on their way called at Miletus, where Paul sent for the elders of the church at Ephesus, and delivered that most solemn and affectionate farewell, recorded in the twentieth chapter of the Acts of the Apostles. From hence they sailed for Tyre, where they tarried seven days and from thence proceeded to Jerusalem.

Paul's fourth and last journey (or rather voyage) was to Rome, where he went in the character of a prisoner. For while being at Jerusalem he was quickly apprehended by the Jews; but being rescued by Lysias, the chief captain, he was sent to Cesarea to take his trial. Here he made his defence before Felix and Drusilla, in such a way that the judge, instead of the prisoner, was made to tremble. Here also he made his defence before Festus, Agrippa, and Bernice, with such force of evidence that Agrippa was almost persuaded to be a Christian. But the malice of the Jews being insatiable, and Paul finding himself in danger of being delivered into their hands, was constrained to appeal unto Caesar. This was the occasion of his being sent to Rome, where he arrived after a long and dangerous voyage, and being shipwrecked on the island of Melita, where he wrought miracles, and Publius, the governor, was converted (*Acts* 21:17–28:10).

When he arrived at Rome he addressed his countrymen the Jews, some of whom believed; but when others rejected the gospel, he turned from them to the Gentiles, and for two whole years dwelt in his own hired house preaching the kingdom of God, and teaching those things which concern the Lord Jesus Christ, with all confidence, no man forbidding him (*Acts* 28:16-31).

Thus far the history of the Acts of the Apostles informs us of the success of the word in the primitive times; and history informs us of its being preached about this time in many other places. Peter speaks of a church at Babylon (*1 Pet.*5:13); Paul proposed a journey to Spain (*Rom.* 15:24), and it is generally believed he went there and likewise came to France and Britain. Andrew preached to the Scythians, north of the Black Sea. John is said to have preached in India, and we know that he was at the Isle of Patmos, in the Archipelago. Philip is reported to have preached in upper Asia, Scythia, and Phrygia; Bartholomew in India, on this side of the Ganges, Phrygia, and Armenia; Matthew in Arabia, or Asiatic Ethiopia, and Parthia; Thomas in India, as far as the coast of Coromandel, and some say in the island of Ceylon; Simon, the Canaanite, in Egypt, Cyrene, Mauritania, Lybia, and other parts of Africa, and from thence to have come to Britain; and Jude is said to have been principally engaged in the lesser Asia and Greece. Their labours were evidently very extensive, and very successful; so that Pliny the Younger, who lived soon after the death of the apostles, in a letter to the emperor Trajan, observed that Christianity had spread not only through towns and cities but also through whole countries. Indeed before this, in the time of Nero, it was so prevalent that it was thought necessary to oppose it by an Imperial Edict, and accordingly the proconsuls, and other governors, were commissioned to destroy it.

Justin Martyr, who lived about the middle of the second century, in his dialogue with Trypho, observed that there was no part of mankind, whether Greeks or barbarians, or any others, by whatever name they were called, whether the Sarmatians, or the Nomades, who had no houses, or the Scenites of Arabia Petrea, who lived in tents among their cattle, where supplications and thanksgivings are not offered up to the Father, and maker of all things, through the name of Jesus Christ. Irenaeus, who lived about the year 170, speaks of churches that were founded in Germany, Spain, France, the eastern countries, Egypt, Lybia, and the middle of the world. Tertullian, who lived and wrote at Carthage in Africa, about twenty years afterwards, enumerating the countries where Christianity had penetrated makes mention of the Parthians, Medes, Elamites, Mesopotamians, Armenians, Phrygians, Cappadocians, the inhabitants of Pontus, Asia, Pamphylia, Egypt, and the regions of Africa beyond Cyrene, the Romans, and Jews, formerly of Jerusalem, many of the Getuli, many borders of the Mauri, or Moors, in Mauritania; now Barbary, Morocco, etc., all the borders of Spain, many nations of the Gauls, and the places in Britain which were inaccessible to the Romans; the Dacians, Sarmatians, Germans, Scythians, and the inhabitants of many hidden nations and provinces, and of many islands unknown to him, and which he could not enumerate. The labours of the ministers of the gospel, in this early period, were so remarkably blessed of God, that the last-mentioned writer observed, in a letter to Scapula, that if he began a persecution the city of Carthage itself must be decimated thereby. Yea, and so abundant were they in the three first centuries, that ten years constant and almost universal persecution under Dioclesian, could neither root out the Christians, nor prejudice their cause.

After this they had great encouragement under several emperors, particularly Constantine and Theodosius, and a very great work of God was carried on; but the ease and affluence which in these times attended the church, served to introduce a flood of corruption, which by degrees brought on the whole system of popery, by means of which all appeared to be lost again; and Satan set up his kingdom of darkness, deceit, and human authority over conscience, through all the Christian world.

In the time of Constantine, one Frumentius was sent to preach to the Indians, and met with great success. A young woman who was a Christian, being taken captive by the Iberians, or Georgians, near the Caspian Sea, informed them of the truths of Christianity, and was so much regarded that they sent to Constantine for ministers to come and preach the word to them. About the same time some barbarous nations having made irruptions into Thrace, carried away several Christians captive, who preached the gospel; by which means the inhabitants upon the Rhine, and the Danube, the Celtae, and some other parts of Gaul, were brought to embrace Christianity. About this time also James of Nisbia, went into Persia to strengthen the Christians, and preach to the heathens; and his success was so great that Adiabene was almost entirely Christian. About the year 372, one Moses, a monk, went to preach to the Saracens, who then lived in Arabia, where he had great success; and at this time the Goths, and other northern nations, had the kingdom of Christ further extended amongst them, but which was very soon corrupted with Arianism.

Soon after this the kingdom of Christ was further extended among the Scythian Nomades, beyond the Danube, and about the year 430, a people called the Burgundians, received the gospel. Four years after that Palladius was sent to preach in Scotland, and the next year Patrick was sent from Scotland to preach to the Irish, who before his time were totally uncivilized, and, some say, cannibals; he however, was useful, and laid the foundations of several churches in Ireland. Presently after this, truth spread further among the Saracens, and in 522, Zathus, king of the Colchians encouraged it, and many of that nation were converted to Christianity. About this same time also the work was extended in Ireland, by Finian, and in Scotland by Constantine and Columba; the latter of whom preached also to the Picts, and Brudaeus, the king, with several others, were converted. About 541, Adad, the king of Ethiopia, was converted by the preaching of Mansionarius; the Heruli beyond the Danube, were now made obedient to the faith, and the Abasgi, near the Caucasian Mountains.

But now popery, especially the compulsive part of it, was risen to such an height, that the usual method of propagating the gospel, or rather what was so called, was to conquer pagan nations by force of arms, and then oblige them to submit to Christianity, after which bishopricks were erected, and persons then sent to instruct the people. I shall just mention some of those who are said to have laboured thus.

In 596, Austin, the monk, Melitus, Justus, Paulinus, and Ruffinian, laboured in England, and in their way were very successful. Paulinus, who appears to have been one of the best of them, had great success in Northumberland; Birinnius preached to the West Saxons, and Felix to the East Angles. In 589, Amandus Gallus laboured in Ghent, Chelenus in Artois, and Gallus and Columbanus in Suabia. In 648, Egidius Gallus in Flanders, and the two Evaldi, in Westphalia. In 684, Willifred, in the Isle of Wight. In 688, Chilianus, in upper Franconia. In 698, Boniface, or Winifred, among the Thuringians, near Erford, in Saxony, and Willibroad in West-Friesland. Charlemagne conquered Hungary in the year 800, and obliged the inhabitants to profess Christianity, when Modestus likewise preached to the Venedi, at the source of the Save and Drave. In 833, Ansgarius preached in Denmark, Gaudibert in Sweden, and about 861, Methodius and Cyril, in Bohemia.

About the year 500, the Scythians over-ran Bulgaria, and Christianity was extirpated; but about 870 they were re-converted. Poland began to be brought over about the same time; and afterwards, about 960 or 990, the work was further extended amongst the Poles and Prussians. The work was begun in Norway in 960, and in Muscovy in 989, the Swedes propagated Christianity in Finland, in 1168, Lithuania became Christian in 1386, and Samogitia in 1439. The Spaniards forced popery upon the inhabitants of South America, and the Portuguese in Asia. The Jesuits were sent into China in 1552. Xavier, whom they call the apostle of the Indians, laboured in the East Indies and Japan, from 1541 to 1552, and several missions of Capauchins were sent to Africa in the seventeenth century. But blind zeal, gross superstition, and infamous cruelties, so marked the appearances of religion all this time, that the professors of Christianity needed conversion, as much as the heathen world.

A few pious people had fled from the general corruption, and lived obscurely in the valleys of Piedmont and Savoy, who were like the seed of the church. Some of them were now and then necessitated to travel into other parts, where they faithfully testified against the corruptions of the times. About 1369 Wickliffe began to preach the faith in England, and his preaching and writings were the means of the conversion of great numbers, many of whom became excellent preachers; and a work was begun which afterwards spread in England, Hungary, Bohemia, Germany, Switzerland, and many other places. John Huss and Jerome of Prague, preached boldly and successfully in Bohemia, and the adjacent parts. In the following century Luther, Calvin, Melanchthon, Bucer, Martyr, and many others, stood up against all the rest of the world; they preached, and prayed, and wrote; and nations agreed one after another to cast off the yoke of popery, and to embrace the doctrine of the gospel.

In England, Episcopal tyranny succeeded to popish cruelty, which, in the year 1620, obliged many pious people to leave their native land and settle in America; these were followed by others in 1629, who laid the foundations of several gospel churches, which have increased amazingly since that time, and the Redeemer has fixed his throne in that country, where but a little time ago, Satan had universal dominion.

In 1632, Mr Elliot, of New England, a very pious and zealous minister, began to preach to the Indians, among whom he had great success; several churches of Indians were planted, and some preachers and school-masters raised up amongst them; since which time others have laboured amongst them with some good encouragement. About the year 1743, Mr David Brainerd was sent a missionary to some more Indians, where he preached and prayed, and after some time an extraordinary work of conversion was wrought, and wonderful success attended his ministry. And at this present time, Mr Kirkland and Mr Sergeant are employed in the same good work, and God has considerably blessed their labours.

In 1706, the king of Denmark sent a Mr Ziegenbalg, and some others, to Tranquebar, on the Coromandel coast in the East Indies, who were useful to the natives, so that many of the heathens were turned to the Lord. The Dutch East India Company likewise having extended their commerce, built the city of Batavia, and a church was opened there; and the Lord's Supper was administered for the first time, on the 3rd of January, 1621, by their minister James Hulzibos, from hence some ministers were sent to Amboyna, who were very successful. A seminary of learning was erected at Leyden, in which ministers and assistants were educated, under the renowned Walaeus, and some years a great number were sent to the East, at the Company's expense, so that in a little time many thousands at Formosa, Malabar, Ternate, Jaffanapatnam, in the town of Columba, at Amboyna, Java, Banda, Macassar, and Malabar, embraced the religion of our Lord Jesus Christ. The work has decayed in some places, but they now have churches in Ceylon, Sumatra, Java, Amboyna, and some other of the spice islands, and at the Cape of Good Hope, in Africa. But none of the moderns have equalled the Moravian Brethren in this good work; they have sent missions to Greenland, Labrador, and several of the West Indian Islands, which have been blessed for good. They have likewise sent to Abyssinia, in Africa, but what success they have had I cannot tell.

The late Mr Wesley lately made an effort in the West Indies, and some of their ministers are now labouring amongst the Caribbs and Negroes, and I have seen pleasing accounts of their success.

SECTION THREE
CONTAINING A SURVEY OF THE PRESENT
STATE OF THE WORLD

In this survey I shall consider the world as divided, according to its usual division, into four parts, *Europe, Asia, Africa,* and *America*, and take notice of the extent of the several countries, their population, civilization, and religion. The article of religion I shall divide into Christian, Jewish, Mahometan, and Pagan; and shall now and then hint at the particular sect of them that prevails in the places which I shall describe. The following Tables will exhibit a more comprehensive view of what I propose, than any thing I can offer on the subject.

EUROPE

| Countries | Extent(miles) | | Number of | Religion |
	Length	Breadth	Inhabitants	
Great Britain	680	300	12,000,000	Protestants, of many denominations
Ireland	285	160	2,000,000	Protestants/Papists
France	600	500	24,000,000	Catholics, Deists, and Protestants
Spain	700	500	9,500,000	Papists
Portugal	300	100	2,000,000	Papists
Sweden, *inc.* Gothland, Shonen, Lapland, Bothnia, and Finland	800	500	3,500,000	The Swedes are serious Lutherans but most of the Laplanders are Pagans and very superstitious

EUROPE

Countries	Extent (miles)		Number of	Religion
	Length	Breadth	Inhabitants	
Isle of Gothland	80	23	5,000	
—Oefel	45	24	2,500	
— Oeland	84	9	1,000	
—Dago	26	23	1,000	
—Aland	24	20	800	
— Hogland	9	5	100	
Denmark	240	114	360,000	Lutherans of the Helvetic Confession
Isle of Zeeland	60	60	284,000	Ditto
— Funen	38	32	144,000	Ditto
— Arroe	8	2	200	Ditto
—Iceland	435	185	60,000	Ditto
— Langeland	27	12	3,000	Ditto
— Laland	38	30	148,000	Ditto
— Falster	27	12	3,000	Ditto
— Mona	14	5	600	Ditto
— Alsen	15	6	600	Ditto
— Femeren	13	8	1,000	Ditto
— Bornholm	20	12	2,000	Lutherans
Greenland	Undiscovered		7,000	Pagans, and Moravian Christians
Norway	750	170	724,000	Lutherans
24 Faro Isles			4,500	Ditto
Danish Lapland	285	172	100,000	Ditto, and Pagans
Poland	700	680	9,000,000	Papists, Lutherans, Calvinists and Jews
Prussia*	400	160	2,500,000	Calvinists, Catholics and Lutherans
Sardinia	135	57	600,000	Papists
Sicily	180	92	1,000,000	Ditto
Italy	660	120	20,000,000	Ditto
United Netherlands	150	150	2,000,000	Protestants of several denominations
Austrian Netherlands	200	200	2,500,000	Papists and Protestants
Switzerland	260	100	2,880,000	Papists and Protestants

* The rest of the Prussian dominions are counted to the countries they lie in.

EUROPE

| COUNTRIES | EXTENT(miles) | | NUMBER OF | RELIGION |
	LENGTH	BREADTH	INHABITANTS	
The Grisons	100	62	800,000	Lutherans/Papists
The Abbacy of St. Gall	24	10	50,000	Ditto
Neufchatel	32	20	100,000	Calvinists
Valais	80	30	440,000	Papists
Piedmont	140	98	900,000	Papists/Protestants
Savoy	87	60	720,000	Ditto
Geneva, City			24,000	Calvinists
Bohemia	478	322	2,100,000	Papists/Moravians
Hungary	300	200	2,500,000	Papists
Germany	600	500	20,000,000	Papists/Protestants
Russia in Europe	1,500	1,100	22,000,000	Greek Church
Turkey in Europe	1,000	900	22,000,000	Greek Christians, Jews, Mahometans
Budziac Tartary	300	60	1,200,000	Ditto
Lesser Tartary	390	65	1,000,000	Ditto
Crim Tartary	145	80	500,000	Ditto
Isle of Tenedos	5	3	200	Mahometans
— Negropont	90	25	25,000	Ditto
— Lemnos	25	25	4,000	Ditto
— Paros	36 in compass		4,500	Greek Christians
— Lesbos, or Mitylene	160 in compass		30,000	Mahometans and Greeks
— Naxia	100 in compass		8,000	Greeks/Papists
— Scio, or Chios	112 in compass		113,000	Greeks/Papists/ Mahometans
— Nio	40 in compass		1,000	Ditto
— Scyros	60 in compass		1,000	Ditto
— Mycone	36 in compass		3,000	Ditto
— Samos	30	15	12,000	Mahometans
— Nicaria	70 in compass		3,000	Greek Christians
— Andros	120 in compass		4,000	Ditto
— Cyclades, *Delos the chief*			700	Ditto
— Zia	40 in compass		8,000	Ditto
— Cerigo, or Cytheraea	50 in compass		1,000	Ditto
— Santorin	36 in compass		10,000	Ditto and Papists
— Policandra	8 in compass		400	Ditto
— Patmos	18 in compass		600	Ditto
— Sephanto	36 in compass		5,000	Greeks
— Claros	40 in compass		1,700	Mahometans

EUROPE

COUNTRIES	EXTENT(miles)		NUMBER OF	RELIGION
	LENGTH	BREADTH	INHABITANTS	
— Amorgo	36 in compass		4,000	Greek Christians
— Leros	18 in compass		800	Christians and Mahometans
— Thermia	40 in compass		6,000	Greek Christians
— Stampalia	50 in compass		3,000	Ditto
— Salamis	50 in compass		1,000	Ditto
— Scarpanta	20 in compass		2,000	Ditto
— Cephalonia	130 in compass		50,000	Ditto
— Zant	50 in compass		30,000	Ditto
— Milo	60 in compass		40,000	Ditto
— Corfu	120 in compass		60,000	Ditto
— Candia, or Crete	200	60	400,000	Greeks/Mahometans
— Coos, or Stanchia	70 in compass		12,800	Ditto
— Rhodes	60	25	120,000	Ditto
— Cyprus	150	70	300,000	Mahometans

ASIA

COUNTRIES	EXTENT(miles)		NUMBER OF	RELIGION
	LENGTH	BREADTH	INHABITANTS	
Turkey in Asia *contains* Anatolia, Syria, Palestine, Diabekr, Turcomania, and Georgia	1,000	800	20,000,000	Mahometanism is most prevalent, but there are many Greek, Latin, Eutychian and Armenian Christians
Arabia	1,300	1,200	16,000,000	Mahometans
Persia	1,280	1,140	20,000,000	Ditto, of the sect of Ali
Great Tartary	4,000	1,200	40,000,000	Mahometan/Pagans
Siberia	2,800	960	7,500,000	Greek Christians/ Pagans
Samojedia	2,000	370	1,900,000	Pagans
Kamtschatcha	540	236	900,000	Ditto
Nova Zembla	*Undiscovered*		Thinly inhabited	Ditto
China	1,400	1,260	60,000,000	Ditto
Japan *contains* Niphon Isle	900	360	10,000,000	Ditto
Isle of Ximo	210	200	3,000,000	Ditto
—Xicoco	117	104	1,800,000	Ditto
— Tsussima	39	34	40,000	Ditto
—Iki	20	17	6,000	Ditto

ASIA

Countries	Extent(miles)		Number of	Religion
	Length	Breadth	Inhabitants	
—Kubitessima	30	26	8,000	Ditto
— Matounsa	54	26	50,000	Ditto
—Fastistia	36	34	30,000	Ditto
—Firando	30	28	10,000	Ditto
— Amacusa	27	24	6,000	Ditto
— Awasi	30	18	5,000	Ditto
India *beyond the* Ganges	2,000	1,000	50,000,000	Mahometans and Pagans
Indostan	2,000	1,500	110,000,000	Ditto
Tibet	1,200	480	10,000,000	Pagans
Isle of Ceylon	250	200	2,000,000	Pagans, except the Dutch Christians
— Maldives	1,000 in number		100,000	Mahometans
— Sumatra	1,000	100	2,100,000	Ditto and Pagan
— Java	580	100	2,700,000	Ditto
— Timor	2,400	54	300,000	Ditto, and a few Christians
— Borneo	800	700	8,000,000	Ditto
—Celebes	510	240	2,000,000	Ditto
— Boutam	75	30	80,000	Mahometans
—Carpentyn	30	3	2,000	Christian Protestants
— Ourature	18	6	3,000	Pagans
—Pullo Lout	60	36	10,000	Ditto

Besides the little islands of Manaar, Aripen, Caradivia, Pengandiva, Analativa, Nainandiva and Nindundiva, which are inhabited by Christian Protestants. And Banca, Madura, Bally, Lambeck, Flores, Solor, Leolana, Panterra, Miscomby, and several others, inhabited by Pagans and Mahometans.

The Moluccas are

— Banda	20	10	6,000	Pagans & Mahometans
— Buro	25	10	7,000	Ditto
— Amboyna	25	10	7,500	Christians; the Dutch have 25 churches
— Ceram	210	45	250,000	Pagans & Mahometans
— Gillola	190	110	650,000	Ditto

And Pullo-way, Pullo-rin, Nera, Guamanapi, Guilliaien, Ternate, Motir, Machian, and Bachian, which are inhabited by Pagans and Mahometans.

Isle of Mindanao	60	40	18,000	Pagans & Mahometans
— Bahol	24	12	6,000	Ditto

ASIA

| COUNTRIES | EXTENT(miles) | | NUMBER OF | RELIGION |
	LENGTH	BREADTH	INHABITANTS	
— Layta	48	27	10,000	Ditto
— Parragon	240	60	100,000	Ditto
The Calamines are				
— Sebu	60	24	10,000	Papists
— Mindora	60	36	12,000	Pagans & Mahometans
— Philippina	185	120	104,000	Ditto
— Negroes Isle	150	60	80,000	Papists
— Manilla			31,000	Ditto and Pagans

The Ladrone Islands are inhabited by most uncivilized Pagans.

New Holland	2,500	2,000	12,000,000	Pagans; 1 or 2 ministers are there.
New Zealand (Two Islands)	960	180	1,120,000	Ditto
New Guinea	1,000	360	1,900,000	Ditto
New Britain	180	120	900,000	Ditto
New Ireland	180	60	700,000	Ditto
Onrong Java	A Cluster of Isles			Ditto
New Caledonia	260	30	170,000	Ditto
New Hebrides				Ditto
Friendly Isles	20 in number			Ditto
Sandwich Isles	7 in number			Ditto
Society Isles	6 in number			Ditto
Kurile Isles	45 in number			Ditto
Pelew Isles				Ditto
Oonalashka Isle	40	20	3,000	Ditto
The other South-Seas Islands				Ditto

AFRICA

| COUNTRIES | EXTENT(miles) | | NUMBER OF | RELIGION |
	LENGTH	BREADTH	INHABITANTS	
Egypt	600	250	2,200,000	Mahometans/Jews
Nubia	940	600	3,000,000	Ditto
Barbary	1,800	500	3,500,000	Ditto, & Christians
Biledulgerid	2,500	350	3,500,000	Ditto
Zaara, or the Desert	3,400	660	800,000	Ditto
Abyssinia	900	800	5,800,000	Armenian Christians
Abex	540	130	1,600,000	Christians/Pagans

AFRICA

COUNTRIES	EXTENT(miles)		NUMBER OF	RELIGION
	LENGTH	BREADTH	INHABITANTS	
Negroland	2,200	840	18,000,000	Pagans
Loango	410	300	1,500,000	Ditto
Congo	540	220	2,000,000	Ditto
Angola	360	250	1,400,000	Ditto
Benguela	430	180	1,600,000	Ditto
Mataman	450	240	1,500,000	Ditto
Ajan	900	300	2,500,000	Ditto
Zanguebar	1,400	350	3,000,000	Ditto
Monoemugi	900	660	2,000,000	Ditto
Sofala	480	300	1,000,000	Ditto
Terra de Natal	600	350	2,000,000	Ditto
Cassraria, or the Hottentots Country	708	660	2,000,000	Ditto, a few Christians at the Cape
I. of Madagascar	1,000	220	2,000,000	Pagans/Mahometans
— St Mary	54	9	5,000	French Papists
—Mascarin	39	30	17,000	Ditto
—St Helena	21 in compass		1,000	English/French Christians
—Annabon	16	14	4,000	Portuguese Papists
—St Thomas	25	23	9,000	Pagans
—Zocotora	80	54	10,000	Mahometans
—Comora Is.	5 in number		5,000	Ditto
—Mauritius	150 in compass		10,000	French Papists
—Bourbon	90 in compass		15,000	Ditto
—Madeiras	3 in number		10,000	Papists
— Cape Verd Is.	10 in number		20,000	Ditto
—Canaries	12 in number		30,000	Ditto
—Azores	9 in number		100,000	Ditto
—Maltha	15	8	1,200	Ditto

AMERICA

COUNTRIES	EXTENT(miles)		NUMBER OF	RELIGION
	LENGTH	BREADTH	INHABITANTS	
All the islands in the Vicinity of Cape Horn				Pagans
The Bermudas extend	16	5	20,000	English/Slaves

AMERICA

| Countries | Extent(miles) | | Number of | Religion |
	Length	Breadth	Inhabitants	
The Little Antilles are				
—Aruba	5	3	200	Dutch/PaganNegroes
—Curassoa	30	10	11,000	Ditto
—Bonaire	10	3	300	Ditto
— Margaritta	40	24	18,000	Spanish/PaganNegroes
—St Trinidad	90	60	100,000	Ditto
The Bahamas are				
—Bahama	50	16	16,000	Pagans
—Providence	28	11	6,000	Ditto

Besides Eluthera, Harbour, Lucayonegua, Andross, Cigateo, Guanaliana, Yumeta, Samana, Yuma, Mayaguana, Ynagua, Caieos and Triangula – Pagans

The Antilles are				
—Cuba	700	60	1,000,000	Papists
—Jamaica	140	60	400,000	English/PaganNegroes
—St Domingo	450	150	1,000,000	French, Spaniards, and Negroes
—Porto Rico	100	49	300,000	Spaniards and Negroes
—Vache or Cows I.	18	2	1,000	Ditto

The Virgin Isles are 12 in number of which Danes Island is the principal – Protestants

Brazil	2,900	900	14,000,000	Pagans/Papists
Paraguay	1,140	460	10,000,000	Pagans
Chile	1,200	500	2,000,000	Pagans/Papists
Peru	1,800	600	10,000,000	Ditto
Country of the Amazons	1,200	900	8,000,000	Pagans
Terra Firma	1,400	700	10,000,000	Pagans/Papists
Guiana	780	480	2,000,000	Ditto
Terra Magellanica	1,400	460	9,000,000	Pagans
Old Mexico	2,220	600	13,500,000	Pagans/Papists
New Mexico	2,000	1,000	14,000,000	Ditto
The States of America	1,000	600	14,000,000	Christians of various denominations

AMERICA

Countries	Extent(miles)		Number of	Religion
	Length	Breadth	Inhabitants	
Terra de 1,680 600			8,000,000	Christians of various
Labrador, Nova Scotia, Louisiana				denominations, but
Canada, and all the country inland				but most N. American
from Mexico to Hudson's Bay				Indians are Pagans.
California, 2,820 1,380			9,000,000	Pagans
and from thence along the Western coast to 70 Degrees				
south latitude and so far inland as to meet the above article.				
All to the north of 70 Degrees unknown				Pagans
Cape Breton 400 110			20,000	Christians
–Newfoundland 350 200			1,400	Protestants
–Cumberland's Is. 780 300			10,000	Pagans
–Madre de Dios 105 30			8,000	Ditto
–Terra del Fuego 120 36			5,000	Ditto
The Caribbees are				
— St Cruz 30 10			13,500	Danish Protestants
— Anguilla 30 9			6,000	Protestants/Negroes
— St Martin 21 12			7,500	Ditto
— St Bartholomew 6 4			720	Ditto
— Barbuda 20 12			7,500	Ditto
— Saba 5 4			1,500	Ditto
— Guardulope 45 38			50,000	Catholics/Pagan Negroes
— Marigalante 15 12			5,400	Ditto
— Tobago 32 9			2,400	Ditto
— Desiada 12 6			1,500	Ditto
— Granada 30 15			13,500	English/Pagan Negroes
— St Lucia 23 12			5,000	Ditto

			Whites	Negroes	
— St Eustatia	6	4	5,000	15,000	Dutch, English, etc.
— St Christopher	20	7	6,000	36,000	English
— Nevis	6	4	5,000	10,000	Ditto
— Antigua	20	20	7,000	30,000	Ditto
— Montserrat	6	6	5,000	10,000	Ditto
— Martinico	60	30	20,000	50,000	French
— St Vincent's	24	18	8,000	5,000	The 8,000 are native Caribbs.
— Barbadoes	21	14	30,000	100,000	English
— Dominica	28	13		40,000	Ditto, 2,000 Native Caribbs.
— St Thomas	15 in compass			8,000	Danish Protestants

This, as nearly as I can obtain information, is the state of the world; though in many countries, as Turkey, Arabia, Great Tartary, Africa, and America, except the United States, and most of the Asiatic Islands, we have no accounts of the number of inhabitants, that can be relied on. I have therefore only calculated the extent, and counted a certain number on an average upon a square mile; in some countries more, and in others less, according as circumstances determine. A few general remarks upon it will conclude this section.

First, the inhabitants of the world according to this calculation, amount to about seven hundred and thirty-one millions; four hundred and twenty millions of whom are still in pagan darkness; an hundred and thirty millions the followers of Mahomet; an hundred millions Catholics; forty-four millions Protestants; thirty millions of the Greek and Armenian churches, and perhaps seven millions of Jews. It must undoubtedly strike every considerate mind, what a vast proportion of the sons of Adam there are, who yet remain in the most deplorable state of heathen darkness, without any means of knowing the true God, except what are afforded them by the works of nature; and utterly destitute of the knowledge of the gospel of Christ, or of any means of obtaining it. In many of these countries they have no written language, consequently no Bible, and are only led by the most childish customs and traditions. Such, for instance, are all the middle and back parts of North America, the inland parts of South America, the South Sea Islands, New Holland, New Zealand, New Guinea; and I may add Great Tartary, Siberia, Samojedia, and the other parts of Asia contiguous to the frozen sea; the greatest part of Africa, the island of Madagascar, and many places beside. In many of these parts also they are cannibals, feeding upon the flesh of their slain enemies, with the greatest brutality and eagerness. The truth of this was ascertained, beyond a doubt, by the late eminent navigator, Cooke, of the New Zealanders, and some of the inhabitants of the western coast of America. Human sacrifices are also very frequently offered, so that scarce a week elapses without instances of this kind. They are in general poor, barbarous, naked pagans, as destitute of civilization, as they are of true religion.

Secondly, barbarous as these poor heathens are, they appear to be as capable of knowledge as we are; and in many places, at least, have discovered uncommon genius and tractableness; and I greatly question whether most of the barbarities practised by them, have not originated in some real or supposed affront, and are therefore, more properly, acts of self-defence, than proofs of inhuman and bloodthirsty dispositions.

Thirdly, in other parts, where they have a written language, as in the East Indies, China, Japan, etc., they know nothing of the gospel. The Jesuits indeed once made many converts to popery among the Chinese; but their highest aim seemed to be to obtain their good opinion; for though the converts professed themselves Christians, yet they were allowed to honour the image of Confucius their great lawgiver; and at length their ambitious intrigues brought upon them the displeasure of government, which terminated in the suppression of the mission, and almost, if not entirely, of the Christian name. It is also a melancholy fact, that the vices of Europeans have been communicated wherever they themselves have been; so that the religious state of even heathens has been rendered worse by intercourse with them!

Fourthly, a very great proportion of Asia and Africa, with some part of Europe, are Mahometans; and those in Persia, who are of the sect of Hali, are the most inveterate enemies to the Turks; and they in return abhor the Persians. The Africans are some of the most ignorant of all the Mahometans; especially the Arabs, who are scattered through all the northern parts of Africa, and live upon the depredations which they are continually making upon their neighbours.

Fifthly, in respect to those who bear the Christian name, a

very great degree of ignorance and immorality abounds amongst them. There are Christians, so called, of the Greek and Armenian churches, in all the Mahometan countries; but they are, if possible, more ignorant and vicious than the Mahometans themselves. The Georgian Christians, who are near the Caspian Sea, maintain themselves by selling their neighbours, relations, and children, for slaves to the Turks and Persians. And it is remarked, that if any of the Greeks of Anatolia turn Muslim, the Turks never set any store by them, on account of their being so much noted for dissimulation and hypocrisy. It is well known that most of the members of the Greek Church are very ignorant. Papists also are in general ignorant of divine things, and very vicious. Nor do the bulk of the Church of England much exceed them, either in knowledge or holiness; and many errors, and much looseness of conduct, are to be found amongst dissenters of all denominations. The Lutherans in Denmark, are much on a par with the ecclesiastics in England; and the face of most Christian countries presents a dreadful scene of ignorance, hypocrisy, and profligacy. Various baneful, and pernicious errors appear to gain ground, in almost every part of Christendom; the truths of the gospel, and even the gospel itself, are attacked, and every method that the enemy can invent is employed to undermine the kingdom of our Lord Jesus Christ.

All these things are loud calls to Christians, and especially to ministers, to exert themselves to the utmost in their several spheres of action, and to try to enlarge them as much as possible.

SECTION FOUR
THE PRACTICABILITY OF SOMETHING BEING DONE, MORE THAN WHAT IS DONE, FOR THE CONVERSION OF THE HEATHEN

The impediments in the way of carrying the gospel among the heathen must arise, I think, from one or other of the following things: either their distance from us, their barbarous and savage manner of living, the danger of being killed by them, the difficulty of procuring the necessaries of life, or the unintelligibleness of their languages.

First, as to their distance from us, whatever objections might have been made on that account before the invention of the mariner's compass, nothing can be alleged for it, with any colour of plausibility in the present age. Men can now sail with as much certainty through the Great South Sea, as they can through the Mediterranean, or any lesser sea. Yea, and providence seems in a manner to invite us to the trial, as there are to our knowledge trading companies, whose commerce lies in many of the places where these barbarians dwell. At one time or other ships are sent to visit places of more recent discovery, and to explore parts of the most unknown; and every fresh account of their ignorance, or cruelty, should call forth our pity, and excite us to concur with providence in seeking their eternal good. Scripture likewise seems to point out this method, 'Surely the Isles shall wait for me; the ships of Tarshish first, to bring my sons from far, their silver, and their gold with them, unto the name of the Lord, thy God' (*Isa.* 60:9). This seems to imply that in the time of the glorious increase of the church, in the latter days, of which the whole chapter is undoubtedly a prophecy, commerce shall subserve the spread of the gospel. The ships of Tarshish were trading vessels, which made voyages for traffic to various parts; thus much therefore must be meant by it, that *navigation*, especially that which is *commercial*, shall be one great mean of carrying on the work of God; and perhaps it may imply that there shall be a very considerable appropriation of wealth to that purpose.

Secondly, as to their uncivilized, and barbarous way of living, this can be no objection to any, except those whose love of ease renders them unwilling to expose themselves to inconveniences for the good of others.

It was no objection to the apostles and their successors, who went among the barbarous *Germans* and *Gauls*, and still more barbarous *Britons*! They did not wait for the ancient inhabitants of these countries to be civilized before they could be Christianized, but went simply with the doctrine of the cross; and Tertullian could boast that 'those parts of Britain which were proof against the Roman armies, were conquered by the gospel of Christ'. It was no objection to an Elliot, or a Brainerd, in later times. They went forth, and encountered every difficulty of the kind, and found that a cordial reception of the gospel produced those happy effects which the longest intercourse with Europeans, without it could never accomplish. It is no objection to commercial men. It only requires that we should have as much love to the souls of our fellow creatures, and fellow sinners, as they have for the profits arising from a few otter-skins, and all these difficulties would be easily surmounted.

After all, the uncivilized state of the heathen, instead of affording an objection *against* preaching the gospel to them, ought to furnish an argument *for* it. Can we as men, or as Christians, hear that a great part of our fellow creatures, whose souls are as immortal as ours, and who are as capable as ourselves, of adorning the gospel, and contributing by their preaching, writings, or practices to the glory of our Redeemer's name, and the good of his church, are enveloped in ignorance and barbarism? Can we hear that they are without the gospel, without government, without laws, and without arts, and sciences; and not exert ourselves to introduce amongst them the sentiments of men, and of Christians? Would not the spread of the gospel be the most effectual means of their civilization? Would not that make them useful members of society? We know that such effects did in a measure follow the aforementioned efforts of Elliot, Brainerd, and others amongst the American Indians; and if similar attempts were made in other parts of the world, and succeeded with a divine blessing (which we have every reason to think they would), might we not expect to see able Divines, or read well-conducted treatises in defence of the truth, even amongst those who at present seem to be scarcely human?

Thirdly, in respect of the danger of being killed by them, it is true that whoever does go must put his life in his hand, and not consult with flesh and blood; but do not the goodness of the cause, the duties incumbent on us as the creatures of God, and Christians, and the perishing state of our fellow men, loudly call upon us to venture all and use every warrantable exertion for their benefit? Paul and Barnabas, who 'hazarded their lives for the name of our Lord Jesus Christ' (*Acts* 15:26), were not blamed as being rash, but commended for so doing, while John Mark who through timidity of mind deserted them in their perilous undertaking, was branded with censure. After all, as has been already observed, I greatly question whether most of the barbarities practised by the savages upon those who have visited them, have not originated in some real or supposed affront, and were therefore, more properly, acts of self-defence, than proofs of ferocious dispositions. No wonder if the imprudence of sailors should prompt them to offend the simple savage, and the offence be resented; but Elliot, Brainerd, and the Moravian missionaries, have been very seldom molested. Nay, in general the heathen have showed a willingness to hear the word; and have principally expressed their hatred of Christianity on account of the vices of nominal Christians.

Fourthly, as to the difficulty of procuring the necessaries of life, this would not be so great as may appear as at first sight; for though we could not procure European food, yet we might procure such as the natives of those countries which we visit, subsist upon themselves. And this would only be passing through what we have virtually engaged in by entering on the ministerial office. A Christian minister is a person who in a peculiar sense is 'not his own' (*1 Cor.* 6:19); he is the 'servant' of God, and therefore ought to be wholly devoted to him. By entering on that sacred office he solemnly undertakes to be always engaged, as much as possible, in the Lord's work, and not to choose his own pleasure, or employment, or pursue the ministry as a something that is to subserve his own ends, or interests, or as a kind of bye-work. He engages to go where God pleases, and to do, or endure what he sees fit to command, or call him to, in the exercise of his function. He virtually bids farewell to friends, pleasures, and comforts, and stands in readiness to endure the greatest sufferings in the work of his Lord, and Master. It is inconsistent for ministers to please themselves with thoughts of a numerous auditory, cordial friends, a civilized country, legal protection, affluence, splendour, or even a competency. The slights, and hatred of men, and even pretended friends, gloomy prisons, and tortures, the society of barbarians of uncouth speech, miserable accommodations in wretched wildernesses, hunger, and thirst, nakedness, weariness, and painfulness, hard work, and but little worldly encouragement, should rather be the objects of their expectation. Thus the apostles acted, in the primitive times, and endured hardness, as good soldiers of Jesus Christ; and though we live in a civilized country where Christianity is protected by law, [and] are not called to suffer these things while we continue here, yet I question whether all are justified in staying here, while so many are perishing without means of grace in other lands. Sure I am that it is entirely contrary to the spirit of the gospel, for its ministers to enter upon it from interested motives, or with great worldly expectations. On the contrary, the commission is a sufficient call to them to venture all, and, like the primitive Christians, go every where preaching the gospel.

It might be necessary, however, for two, at least, to go together, and in general I should think it best that they should be married men, and to prevent their time from being employed in procuring necessaries, two, or more, other persons, with their wives and families, might also accompany them, who should be wholly employed in providing for them.

In most countries it would be necessary for them to cultivate a little spot of ground just for their support, which would be a resource to them, whenever their supplies failed. Not to mention the advantages they would reap from each others company, it would take off the enormous expense which has always attended undertakings of this kind, the first expense being the whole; for though a large colony needs support for a considerable time, yet so small a number would, upon receiving the first crop, maintain themselves.

They would have the advantage of choosing their situation, their wants would be few; the women, and even the children, would be necessary for domestic purposes; and a few articles of stock, as a cow or two, and a bull, and a few other cattle of both sexes, a very few utensils of husbandry, and some corn to sow their land, would be sufficient. Those who attend the missionaries should understand husbandry, fishing, fowling, etc., and be provided with the necessary implements for these purposes. Indeed a variety of methods may be thought of, and when once the work is undertaken, many things will suggest themselves to us, of which we at present can form no idea.

Fifthly, as to learning their languages, the same means would be found necessary here as in trade between different nations. In some cases interpreters might be obtained, who might be employed for a time; and where these were not to be found, the missionaries must have patience, and mingle with the people, till they have learned so much of their language as to be able to communicate their ideas to them in it. It is well known to require no very extraordinary talents to learn, in the space of a year, or two at most, the language of any people upon earth, so much of it at least, as to be able to convey any sentiments we wish to their understandings.

The missionaries must be men of great piety, prudence, courage, and forbearance; of undoubted orthodoxy in their sentiments, and must enter with all their hearts into the spirit of their mission; they must be willing to leave all the comforts of life behind them, and to encounter all the hardships of a torrid, or frigid climate, an uncomfortable manner of living, and every other inconvenience that can attend this undertaking.

Clothing, a few knives, powder and shot, fishing tackle, and the articles of husbandry above-mentioned, must be provided for them; and when arrived at the place of their destination, their first business must be to gain some acquaintance with the language of the natives (for which purpose two would be better than one), and by all lawful means to endeavour to cultivate a friendship with them, and as soon as possible let them know the errand for which they were sent. They must endeavour to convince them that it was their good alone, which induced them to forsake their friends, and all the comforts of their native country.

They must be very careful not to resent injuries which may be offered to them, nor to think highly of themselves, so as to despise the poor heathens, and by those means lay a foundation for their resentment, or rejection of the gospel. They must take every opportunity of doing them good, and labouring, and travelling, night and day, they must instruct, exhort, and rebuke, with all long suffering, and anxious desire for them, and, above all, must be instant in prayer for the effusion of the Holy Spirit upon the people of their charge. Let but missionaries of the above description engage in the work, and we shall see that it is not impracticable.

It might likewise be of importance, if God should bless their labours, for them to encourage any appearances of gifts amongst the people of their charge; if such should be raised up many advantages would be derived from their knowledge of the language, and customs of their countrymen; and their change of conduct would give great weight to their ministrations.

SECTION FIVE

AN ENQUIRY INTO THE DUTY OF CHRISTIANS IN GENERAL, AND WHAT MEANS OUGHT TO BE USED, IN ORDER TO PROMOTE THIS WORK

If the prophecies concerning the increase of Christ's kingdom be true, and if what has been advanced, concerning the commission given by him to his disciples being obligatory on us, be just, it must be inferred that all Christians ought heartily to concur with God in promoting his glorious designs, for 'he that is joined to the Lord is one Spirit' (*1 Cor.* 6:17).

One of the first, and most important of those duties which are incumbent upon us, is *fervent and united prayer*. However the influence of the Holy Spirit may be set at naught, and run down by many, it will be found upon trial, that all means which we can use, without it, will be ineffectual. If a temple is raised for God in the heathen world, it will not be 'by might, nor by power', nor by the authority of the magistrate, or the eloquence of the orator; 'but by my Spirit, saith the LORD of hosts' (*Zech.* 4:6). We must therefore be in real earnest in supplicating his blessing upon our labours.

It is represented in the prophets, that when there shall be 'a great mourning in the land, as the mourning of Hadadrimmon in the valley of Megiddon, and every family shall mourn apart, and their wives apart', it shall all follow upon 'a spirit of grace, and supplication'. And when these things shall take place, it is promised that 'there shall be a fountain opened for the house of David, and for the inhabitants of Jerusalem, for sin, and for uncleanness,' and that 'the idols shall be destroyed', and 'the false prophets ashamed' of their profession (*Zech.* 12:10,14; 13:1,6). This prophecy seems to teach that when there shall be a universal conjunction in fervent prayer, and all shall esteem Zion's welfare as their own, then copious influences of the Spirit shall be shed upon the churches, which like a purifying *fountain* shall cleanse the servants of the Lord. Nor shall this cleansing influence stop here; all old idolatrous prejudices shall be rooted out, and truth prevail so gloriously that false teachers shall be so ashamed as rather to wish to be classed with obscure herdsmen, or the meanest peasants, than bear the ignominy attendant on their detection.

The most glorious works of grace that have ever took place, have been in answer to prayer; and it is in this way, we have the greatest reason to suppose, that the glorious outpouring of the Spirit, which we expect at last, will be bestowed.

With respect to our own immediate connections, we have within these few years been favoured with some tokens for good, granted in answer to prayer, which should encourage us to persist, and increase in that important duty. I trust our *monthly prayer meetings* for the success of the gospel have not been in vain. It is true a want of importunity too generally attends our prayers; yet unimportunate, and feeble as they have been, it is to be believed that God has heard, and in a measure answered them. The churches that have engaged in the practice have in general since that time been evidently on the increase; some controversies which have long perplexed and divided the church, are more clearly stated than ever; there are calls to preach the gospel in many places where it has not been usually published; yea, a glorious door is opened, and is likely to be opened wider and wider, by the spread of civil and religious liberty, accompanied also by a diminution of the spirit of popery; a noble effort has been made to abolish the inhuman Slave Trade, and though at present it has not been so successful as might be wished, yet it is to be hoped it will be persevered in, till it is accomplished.

In the meantime it is a satisfaction to consider that the late defeat of the abolition of the Slave Trade has proved the occasion of a praiseworthy effort to introduce a free settlement, at Sierra Leone, on the coast of Africa; an effort which, if succeeded with a divine blessing, not only promises to open a way for honourable commerce with that extensive country, and for the civilization of its inhabitants, but may prove the happy means of introducing amongst them the gospel of our Lord Jesus Christ.

These are events that ought not to be overlooked; they are not to be reckoned small things; and yet perhaps they are small compared with what might have been expected, if all had cordially entered into the spirit of the proposal, so as to have made the cause of Christ their own, or in other words to have been so solicitous about it, as if their own advantage depended upon its success. If a holy solicitude had prevailed in all the assemblies of Christians in behalf of their Redeemer's kingdom, we might probably have seen before now, not only an 'open door' (2 *Cor.* 2:12) for the gospel, but 'many running to and fro' (*Dan.* 12:4), and knowledge increased; or a diligent use of those means which providence has put in our power, accompanied with a greater blessing than ordinary from heaven.

Many can do nothing but pray, and prayer is perhaps the only thing in which Christians of all denominations can cordially, and unreservedly unite; but in this we may all be one, and in this the strictest unanimity ought to prevail. Were the whole body thus animated by one soul, with what pleasure would Christians attend on all the duties of religion, and with what delight would their ministers attend on all the business of their calling. We must not be contented however with praying, without exerting ourselves in the use of means for the obtaining of those things we pray for. Were 'the children of light', but 'as wise in their generation as the children of this world' (*Luke* 16:8), they would stretch every nerve to gain so glorious a prize, nor ever imagine that it was to be obtained in any other way.

When a trading company have obtained their charter they usually go to its utmost limits; and their flocks, their ships, their officers, and men are so chosen, and regulated, as to be likely to answer their purpose; but they do not stop here, for encouraged by the prospect of success, they use every effort, cast their bread upon the waters, cultivate friendship with everyone from whose information they expect the least advantage. They cross the widest and most tempestuous seas, and encounter the most unfavourable climates; they introduce themselves into the most barbarous nations, and sometimes undergo the most affecting hardships; their minds continue in a state of anxiety, and suspense, and a longer delay than usual in the arrival of their vessels agitates them with a thousand changeful thoughts, and foreboding apprehensions, which continue till the rich returns are safe arrived in port. But why these fears? Whence all these disquietudes, and this labour? Is it not because their souls enter into the spirit of the project, and their happiness in a manner depends on its success? Christians are a body whose truest interest lies in the exaltation of the Messiah's kingdom. Their charter is very extensive, their encouragements exceeding great, and the returns promised infinitely superior to all the gains of the most lucrative fellowship. Let then everyone in his station consider himself as bound to act with all his might, and in every possible way for God.

Suppose a company of serious Christians, ministers and private persons, were to form themselves into a society, and make a number of rules respecting the regulation of the plan, and the persons who are to be employed as missionaries, the means of defraying the expense, etc., etc. This society must consist of persons whose hearts are in the work, men of serious religion, and possessing a spirit of perseverance; there must be a determination not to admit any person who is not of this description, or to retain him longer than he answers to it.

From such a society a committee might be appointed, whose business it should be to procure all the information they could upon the subject, to receive contributions, to enquire into the characters, tempers, abilities and religious views of the missionaries, and also to provide them with necessaries for their undertakings.

They must also pay a great attention to the views of those who undertake this work; for want of this the missions to the Spice Islands, sent by the Dutch East India Company, were soon corrupted, many going more for the sake of settling in a place where temporal gain invited them, than of preaching to the poor Indians. This soon introduced a number of indolent, or profligate persons, whose lives were a scandal to the doctrines which they preached; and by means of whom the gospel was ejected from Ternate, in 1694, and Christianity fell into great disrepute in other places.

If there is any reason for me to hope that I shall have any influence upon any of my brethren, and fellow Christians, probably it may be more especially amongst them of my own denomination. I would therefore propose that such a society and committee should be formed amongst the Particular Baptist denomination.

I do not mean by this, in any wise to confine it to one denomination of Christians. I wish with all my heart that everyone who loves our Lord Jesus Christ in sincerity, would in some way or other engage in it. But in the present divided state of Christendom, it would be more likely for good to be done by each denomination engaging separately in the work, than if they were to embark in it conjointly. There is room enough for us all, without interfering with each other; and if no unfriendly interference took place, each denomination would bear good will to the other, and wish, and pray for its success, considering it as upon the whole friendly to the great cause of true religion; but if all were intermingled, it is likely their private discords might throw a damp upon their spirits, and much retard their public usefulness.

In respect to *contributions* for defraying the expenses, money will doubtless be wanting; and suppose the rich were to embark a portion of that wealth over which God has made them stewards, in this important undertaking, perhaps there are few ways that would turn to a better account at last. Nor ought it to be confined to the rich; if persons in more moderate circumstances were to devote a portion, suppose a tenth of their annual increase to the Lord, it would not only correspond with the practice of the Israelites, who lived under the Mosaic economy, but of the patriarchs Abraham, Isaac, and Jacob, before that dispensation commenced. Many of our most eminent forefathers amongst the Puritans followed that practice; and if that were but attended to now, there would not only be enough to support the ministry of the gospel at home, and to encourage *village preaching* in our respective neighbourhoods, but to defray the expenses of carrying the gospel into the heathen world.

If congregations were to open subscriptions of *one penny* or more per week, according to their circumstances, and deposit it as a fund for the propagation of the gospel, much might be raised in this way. By such simple means they might soon have it in their power to introduce the preaching of the gospel into most of the villages in England; where, though men are placed whose business it should be to give light to those who sit in darkness, it is well-known that they have it not. Where there was no person to open his house for the reception of the gospel, some other building might be procured for a small sum, and even then something considerable might be spared for the Baptist, or other committees, for propagating the gospel amongst the heathen.

Many persons have of late left off the use of West Indian sugar on account of the iniquitous manner in which it is obtained. Those families who have done so, and have not substituted anything else in its place, have not only cleansed their hands of blood, but have made a saving to their families, some of six pence, and some of a shilling a week. If this or a part of this were appropriated to the uses before-mentioned, it would abundantly suffice. We have only to keep the end in view, and have our hearts thoroughly engaged in the pursuit of it, and means will not be very difficult.

We are exhorted 'to lay up treasure in heaven, where neither moth nor rust doth corrupt, nor thieves break through and steal' (*Matt.* 6:19). It is also declared that 'whatsover a man soweth, that shall he also reap' (*Gal.* 6:7). These Scriptures teach us that the enjoyments of the life to come, bear a near relation to that which now is; a relation similar to that of the harvest, and the seed. It is true all the reward is of mere grace, but it is nevertheless encouraging; what a 'treasure', what a 'harvest' must await such characters as Paul, and Elliot, and Brainerd, and others, who have given themselves wholly to the work of the Lord. What a heaven will it be to see the many myriads of poor heathens, of Britons, amongst the rest, who by their labours have been brought to the knowledge of God. Surely a 'crown of rejoicing' (*1 Thess.* 2:19) like this is worth aspiring to. Surely it is worth while to lay ourselves out with all our might, in promoting the cause, and kingdom of Christ.

FINIS

PART 3

ON DELAY IN RELIGIOUS CONCERNS

Andrew Fuller

1791

THE INSTANCES, THE EVIL NATURE, AND THE DANGEROUS TENDENCY OF DELAY, IN THE CONCERNS OF RELIGION

A sermon preached by Andrew Fuller at a Ministers' Meeting, held at Clipstone, April 27, 1791.[1]

'Thus speaketh the LORD of hosts, saying, This people say, The time is not come, the time that the LORD's house should be built' (*Hag.* 1:2).

W hen the children of Judah were delivered from their captivity, and allowed, by the proclamation of Cyrus, to return to their own land, one of the principal things which attracted their attention was the rebuilding of the house of God, which had been destroyed by the Babylonians. This was a work which Cyrus himself enjoined, and upon which the hearts of the people were fixed. It was not, however, to be accomplished at once; and as the worship of God was a matter of immediate and indispensable concern, they set up an *altar*, on which to offer sacrifices and offerings, till such time as the temple should be built.

In the second year after their return, the foundation of the Lord's house was laid; but opposition being made to it, by the adversaries of Judah and Benjamin, the work ceased all the days of Cyrus, until the reign of Darius, commonly distinguished by the name of Darius Hystaspes. During this period, which seems to have been about fourteen years, the people sunk into a spirit of indifference. At first they desisted from necessity; but afterwards, their attention being turned to the

---

[1] Taken from *The Complete Works of Andrew Fuller* (London: Henry G. Bohn, 1853. Biblical references have been inserted and the spelling slightly modernized.

building and ornamenting of houses for themselves, they seemed very well contented that the house of the Lord should lie waste. For this their temper and conduct the land was smitten with barrenness; so that both the vintage and the harvest failed them. God also raised up Haggai and Zechariah to go and remonstrate against their supineness; and the efforts of these two prophets were the means of stirring up the people to resume the work.

The argument which the people used against building the house of God was that *the time was not come*. It is possible they waited for a counter-order from the Persian court; if so, they might have waited long enough. A work of that nature ought to have been prosecuted of their own accord; at least they should have tried. It did not follow, because they were hindered once, that therefore they should never succeed. Or perhaps they meant to plead their present weakness and poverty. Something like this seems to be implied in the fourth verse, where they are reminded that they had strength enough to build and ornament houses for themselves. It looks as if they wished to build, and lay by fortunes for themselves and their families, and *then*, at some *future* time, they might contribute for the building of the house of God.

There is something of this procrastinating spirit that runs through a great part of our life, and is of great detriment to us in the work of God. We know of many things that should be done, and cannot in conscience directly oppose them; but still we find excuses for our inactivity. While we admit that many things should be done which are not done, we are apt to quiet ourselves with the thought that they need not be done *just now*: 'The time is not come, the time that the LORD's house should be built.'

In discoursing to you upon the subject, brethren, I shall take notice of a few of the most remarkable cases in which this spirit is discovered; and then endeavour to show its evil nature and dangerous tendency.

1. IN RESPECT TO THE CASES, OR INSTANCES, IN WHICH IT IS DISCOVERED.

A small degree of observation on mankind, and of reflection upon the workings of our own hearts, will furnish us with many of these; and convince us of its great influence on every description of men, in almost all their religious concerns.

i. It is by this plea that *a great part of mankind are constantly deceiving themselves in respect to a serious attention to the concerns of their souls*. These are, doubtless, of the last importance; and there are times in which most men not only acknowledge this truth, but, in some sort, feel the force of it. This is the case, especially, with those who have had a religious education, and have been used to attend upon the preaching of the gospel. They hear from the pulpit that men must be born again, must be converted, and become as little children, or never enter into the kingdom of God. Or the same things are impressed upon them by some threatening affliction or alarming providence. They feel themselves at those times very unhappy; and it is not unusual for them to resolve upon a sacrifice of their former sins, and a serious and close attention in future to the affairs of their souls. They think, while under these impressions, they *will* consider their ways, they *will* enter their closets, and shut to the door, and pray to the Lord that he would have mercy upon them; but, alas! no sooner do they retire from the house of God, or recover from their affliction, than the impression begins to subside, and then matters of this sort become less welcome to the mind. They must not be utterly rejected; but are let alone *for the present*. As conscience becomes less alarmed, and danger is viewed at a greater distance, the sinner, by degrees, recovers himself from his fright, and dismisses his religious concern, in some such manner as Felix did his reprover, 'Go thy way for this time, when I have a convenient season I will call for thee' (*Acts* 24:25).

It is thus with the ardent *youth*; in the hour of serious reflection, he feels that religion is of importance; but his heart, still averse from what his conscience recommends, rises against the thought of sacrificing the prime of life to the gloomy duties of prayer and self-denial. He does not resolve *never* to attend to these things; but the *time* does not seem to be come. He hopes that the Almighty will excuse him a *few years*, at least, and impute his excesses to youthful folly and imbecility. It is thus with the *man of business*; there are times in which he is obliged to retire from the hurry of life; and, at those times, thoughts of another life may arrest his attention. Conscience at those intervals may smite him for his living without prayer, without reflection, without God in all his thoughts; and what is his remedy? Does he lament his sin, and implore mercy through our Lord Jesus Christ? No, nor so much as promise to forsake it *immediately*; but *this* he promises, that when *this* busy time is over, and *that* favourite point is gained, and *those* intricate affairs are terminated, *then* it shall be otherwise. It is thus with persons in *single life*: they will be better when they get settled in the world. It is thus with the *encumbered parent*: she looks forward to the time when her family shall get off her hands. It is thus with the *drunkard* and the *debauchee*: wearied in their own way, they intend to lead a new life as soon as they can but shake off their old connexions. In short, it is thus with great numbers in all our towns, and villages, and congregations: they put off the great concern to *another time*, and think they may venture at least a little longer, till all is over with them, and a dying hour just awakens them, like the virgins in the parable, to bitter reflection on their own fatal folly.

ii. This plea not only affects the unconverted, but *prevents us all from undertaking any great or good work for the cause of Christ, or the good of mankind*. We see many things that should be done; but there are difficulties in the way, and we wait for the removal of these difficulties. We are very apt to indulge a kind of prudent caution, (as we call it,) which foresees and magnifies difficulties beyond what they really are. It is granted there may be such things in the way of an undertaking as may render it impracticable; and, in that case, it is our duty for the present to stand still; but it becomes us to beware lest we account that impracticable which only requires such a degree of exertion as we are not inclined to give it. Perhaps the work requires *expense*; and Covetousness says, Wait a little longer, till I have gained so and so in trade, till I have rendered my circumstances respectable, and settled my children comfortably in the world. But is not this like ceiling our own houses, while the house of God lies waste? Perhaps it requires *concurrence*; and we wait for everybody to be of a mind, which is never to be expected. He who through a dread of opposition and reproach desists from known duty is in danger of being found among the 'fearful, the unbelieving, and the abominable' (*Rev.* 21:8).

Had Luther and his contemporaries acted upon this principle, they had never gone about the glorious work of the Reformation. When he saw the abominations of popery, he might have said, 'These things ought not to be; but what can *I* do? If the chief priests and rulers in different nations would but unite, something might be effected; but what can *I* do, an individual, and a poor man? I may render myself an object of persecution, or, which is worse, of universal contempt; and what good end will be answered by it?' Had Luther reasoned thus – had he fancied that, because princes and prelates were not the first to engage in the good work, therefore the time was not come to build the house of the Lord – the house of the Lord, for any thing he had done, might have lain waste to this day.

Instead, of waiting for the removal of difficulties, we ought in many cases, to consider them as purposely laid in our way, in order to try the sincerity of our religion. He who had all power in heaven and earth could not only have sent forth his apostles into all the world, but have so ordered it that all the world should treat them with kindness, and aid them in their mission; but, instead of that, he told them to lay their accounts with persecution and the loss of all things. This was no doubt to try their sincerity; and the difficulties laid in our way are equally designed to try ours.

Let it be considered whether it is not owing to this principle that so few and so feeble efforts have been made for the propagation of the gospel in the world. When the Lord Jesus commissioned his apostles, he commanded them to go and teach 'all nations', to preach the gospel to 'every creature'; and that notwithstanding the difficulties and oppositions that would lie in the way. The apostles executed their commission with assiduity and fidelity; but, since their days, we seem to sit down half contented that the greater part of the world should still remain in ignorance and idolatry. Some noble efforts have indeed been made; but they are small in number, when compared with the magnitude of the object. And why is it so? Are the souls of men of less value than heretofore? No. Is Christianity less true or less important than in former ages? This will not be pretended. Are there no opportunities for societies, or individuals, in Christian nations, to convey the gospel to the heathens? This cannot be pleaded so long as opportunities are found to trade with them, yea, and (what is a disgrace to the name of Christians) to buy them, and sell them, and treat them with worse than savage barbarity! We have opportunities in abundance: the improvement of navigation, and the maritime and commercial turn of this country, furnish us with these; and it deserves to be considered whether this is not a circumstance that renders it a duty peculiarly binding on us.

The truth is, if I am not mistaken, we wait for we know not what; we seem to think 'the time is not come, the time for the Spirit to be poured down from on high'. We *pray* for the conversion and salvation of the world, and yet *neglect the ordinary means* by which those ends have been used to be accomplished. It pleased God, heretofore, by the foolishness of preaching, to save them that believed; and there is reason to think it will still please God to work by that distinguished means. Ought we not then at least to try by some means to convey more of the good news of salvation to the world around us than has hitherto been conveyed? The encouragement to the heathen is still in force, '*Whosoever shall call upon the name of the Lord shall be saved.*' But, 'how shall they call on him in whom they have not believed? and how shall they believe in him of whom they have not heard? and how shall they hear without a preacher? and how shall they preach except they be sent?' (*Rom.* 10:13–15).

Let it be further considered whether it is not owing to this principle that so few and so feeble efforts are made for the propagation of the gospel *in places within our reach*. There are many dark places in our own land-places where priests and people, it is to be feared, are alike destitute of true religion, '*all looking to their own way*, every one for *his gain, from his quarter*' (*Isa.* 56:11). Were every friend of Jesus Christ to avail himself of that liberty which the laws of his country allow him, and embrace every opportunity for the dissemination of evangelical principles, what effects might we hope to see! Were every true minister of the gospel to make a point of preaching as often as possible in the villages within his reach; and did those private Christians who are situated in such villages open their doors for preaching, and recommend the gospel by a holy and affectionate behaviour, might we not hope to see the wilderness become as a fruitful field? Surely, in these matters, we are too negligent. And when we do preach to the unconverted, we do not feel as if we were to do any good. We are as if we knew not how to get at the hearts and consciences of people. We cast the net, without so much as expecting a draught. We are as those who cannot find their hands in the day of battle, who go forth not like men accustomed to conquest, but rather like those inured to defeat. Whence arises all this? Is it not owing, at least a considerable degree of it, to a notion we have that *the time is not come* for any thing considerable to be effected?

iii. It is this plea that keeps many from *a public profession of religion by a practical acknowledgment of Christ*. Christ requires of his followers that they confess his name before men; that they be baptized, and commemorate his dying love in the ordinance of the supper. Yet there are many who consider themselves as Christians, and are considered so by others, who still live in the neglect of these ordinances. I speak not now of those who consider themselves as having been baptized in their infancy, but of such as admit the immersion of believers to be the only true baptism, and yet do not practise it, nor hold communion with any particular church of Christ. It is painful to think there should be a description of professed Christians who live in the neglect of Christ's commands. What can be the motives of such neglect? Probably they are various; there is one, however, that must have fallen under your observation; that is, *the want of some powerful impression upon the mind, impelling them, as it were, to a compliance*. Many persons wait for something of this sort; and because they go from year to year without it, conclude that *the time is not come;* or that it is not the mind of God that they should comply with those ordinances; at least, that they should comply with them *at present*. Impressions, it is allowed, are desirable, provided it be truth or duty that is impressed; otherwise they deserve no regard; but be they as desirable as they may, the want of them can never justify our living in the neglect of known duty. Nor are they at all adapted to show us *what is duty*, but merely to excite to the performance of that which may be proved to be duty without them. We might as well wait for impressions, and conclude, from the want of them, that the time is not come for the performance of other duties as those of baptism and the Lord's supper.

Some are kept from a public profession of Christ's name by mere mercenary motives. They have relations and friends that would be offended. The fear of being disinherited, or injured, in some sort, as to worldly circumstances, has made many a person keep his principles to himself, till such time as the party whose displeasure he fears shall be removed out of the way. This is wicked; as it amounts to a denial of Christ before men, and will, no doubt, expose the party, if he die without repentance for it, to be denied by Christ before his Father at the last day. 'Lord,' said one, 'I will follow thee, but let me first go and bury my father' – 'Let me first go and bid them farewell who are at home', says another: 'Jesus answered, Let the dead bury their dead, follow thou me.' – 'No man having put his hand to the plough, and looking back, is fit for the kingdom of God' (cf. *Luke 9:59–62*).

iv. It is this plea that keeps us from *a thorough self-examination and self-denial*. The importance of being right in the sight of God, and our liability to err, even in the greatest of all concerns, render a close and frequent inquiry into our spiritual state absolutely necessary. It is a dangerous, as well as an uncomfortable life, to be always in suspense; not knowing what nor where we are, nor whither we are going. There are seasons, too, in which we feel the importance of such an inquiry, and think we *will* go about it, we *will* search and try our ways, and turn from our sins, and walk more closely with God. Such thoughts will occur when we hear matters urged home upon us from the pulpit, or when some affecting event draws off our attention from the present world, and causes us to reflect upon ourselves for our inordinate anxiety after it. We think of living otherwise than we have done; but when we come to put our thoughts into execution, we find a number of difficulties in the way, which too often deter us, at least *for the present*. – Here is an undertaking that must first be accomplished, before I can *have time*; here is also a troublesome affair that I must get through, before I can *be composed*; and then here are such temptations that I know not how to get over *just now*: if I wait a little longer, perhaps they may be removed. Alas! alas! thus we befool ourselves; thus we defer it to another time, till the impressions on our minds are effaced, and then we are less able to attend to those things than we were at first. As one who puts off the examination of his accounts, and the retrenchment of his expenses, till, all on a sudden, he is involved in a bankruptcy; so do multitudes, in the religious world, neglect a close inspection into the concerns of their souls, till, at length, either a departure from some of the great principles of the gospel, or some foul and open fall, is the consequence.

v. It is this principle that keeps us from *preparedness for death, and thus being ready when our Lord shall come.* There is nothing that Christ has more forcibly enjoined than this duty: 'Be ye also ready, for at such an hour as ye think not the Son of man cometh' (*Matt.* 24:44). 'What I say unto you I say unto all, Watch' (*Mark* 13:37). Why do we not immediately feel the force of these charges, and betake ourselves to habitual watchfulness, and prayer, and self-denial, and walking with God? Why are we not as men who wait for the coming of their Lord? Is it not from a secret thought that *the time is not come?* We know we must die, but we consider it as something at a distance; and thus, imagining that our Lord delayeth his coming, we delay to prepare to meet him, so that when he cometh he findeth us in confusion. Instead of our loins being girt, and our lights burning, we are engaged in a number of plans and pursuits, to the neglect of those things which, nothwithstanding the necessary avocations of life, ought always to engross our supreme attention.

Let us next proceed to consider:

2. THE EVIL NATURE AND DANGEROUS TENDENCY OF THIS PROCRASTINATING TEMPER.

I need not say much to prove to you that it is a sin. The

conscience of every one of you will assist me in that part of the work. It is proper, however, in order that you may feel it the more forcibly, that you should consider wherein its evil nature consists.

i. It is *contrary to the tenor of all God's commandments*. All through the Scriptures we are required to attend to divine things immediately, and without delay. 'Work while it is called today; the night cometh when no man can work.' – 'Today, if ye will hear his voice, harden not your hearts' (*Heb.* 3:8,15). – 'While ye have light, believe in the light, that ye may be the children of light' (*John* 12:36). – 'Whatsoever thy hand findeth to do, do it with thy might; for there is no work, nor device, nor knowledge, nor wisdom, in the grave, whither thou goest' (*Eccles.* 9:10).

God not only requires us, in general, to do what we do quickly, but calls us to serve him particularly *under those temptations or afflictions* which we find placed in our way. The terms of discipleship are, 'Deny thyself; take up thy cross, and follow me' (*Matt.* 16:24). He does not call upon us to follow him barely when there are no troubles nor difficulties to encounter, nor allow us, when those difficulties occur, to wait a fairer opportunity; but to take our cross, as it were, upon our shoulders, and *so* follow him. It would be of use for us to consider every situation as a post in which God has placed us, and *in which* he calls upon us to serve and glorify him. If we are poor, we are required to glorify God by contentment; if afflicted, by patience; if bereaved, by submission; if persecuted, by firmness; if injured, by forgiveness; or if tempted, by denying ourselves for his sake. Nor can these duties be performed at other times; to put them off, therefore, to another opportunity, is the same thing, in effect, as refusing to comply with them at all.

ii. To put off things to another time *implies a lurking dislike to the things themselves*. We do not ordinarily do so, except in things wherein we have no delight. Whatever our hearts are set upon, we are for losing no time till it is accomplished. If the people of Judah had 'had a mind to work', as is said of them on another occasion, they would not have pleaded that the time was not come. Sinful delay, therefore, arises from *alienation of heart from God,* than which nothing can be more offensive in his sight.

But, further, it is not only a sin, but a sin of *dangerous tendency.* This is manifest by the effects it produces. Precious time is thereby murdered, and valuable opportunities lost, and lost beyond recall!

That there are opportunities possessed, both by saints and sinners, is plain from the Scriptures. The former might do abundantly more for God than they do, and might enjoy much more of God and heaven than they actually enjoy; and no doubt it would be so, were it not for that idle, delaying temper, of which we have spoken. Like the Israelites, we are slothful to go up to possess the good land. Many are the opportunities, both of doing and enjoying good, that have already passed by. Oh, what Christians might we have been before now, had we but availed ourselves of all those advantages which the gospel dispensation and the free exercise of our religion afford us!

Sinners also, as long as life lasts, have opportunity of escaping from the wrath to come. Hence they are exhorted to 'seek the LORD while he may be found', and to 'call upon him while he is near' (*Isa.* 55:6). Hence, also, there is a 'door' represented as being, at present, 'open'; which 'the master of the house' will one day 'rise up and shut' (*Luke* 13:25). The 'fountain' is described as being, at present, 'open for sin and for uncleanness' (*Zech.* 13:1), but there is a period approaching when it shall be said, 'He that is filthy, let him be filthy still!' (*Rev.* 22:11). It seems scarcely in the power of language to express the danger of delay in terms more forcible and impressive than those which are used in the above passages. Nor is there any thing in the idea that clashes with the Scripture doctrine of *decrees.* All allow that men have opportunity, in natural things, to do what they do not, and to obtain what they obtain not; and if this can be made to consist with a universal providence, which 'performeth the things that are appointed for us' (*Job* 23:14), why should not the other be allowed to consist with the purposes of Him who does nothing without a plan, but 'worketh all things after the counsel of his own will' (*Eph.* 1:11)? A price is in the hands of those who have no heart to get wisdom.

O thoughtless sinner! trifle no longer with the murder of time, so short and uncertain in its duration; the morning of your existence; the mould in which you receive an impression for eternity; the only period in which the Son of man has power to forgive sins! Should the remaining part of your life pass away in the same careless manner as that has which has already elapsed, what bitter reflection must needs follow! How cutting it must be to look back on all the means of salvation as gone for ever; the harvest past, the summer ended, and you not saved!

Suppose a company, at the time of low water, should take an excursion upon the sands near the sea-shore: suppose yourself of the company: suppose that, on a presumption of the tide's not returning at present, you should all fall asleep: suppose all the company, except yourself, to awake out of their sleep, and, finding their danger, endeavour to *awake* you, and to persuade you to flee with them for your life; but you, like the sluggard, are for 'a little more sleep, and a little more slumber' (*Prov.* 6:10): the consequence is, your companions escape, but you are left behind to perish in the waters, which, regardless of all your cries, rise and overwhelm you! What a situation would this be! How would you curse that love of sleep that made you refuse to be awaked – that delaying temper that wanted to indulge a little longer! But what is this situation compared with that of a lost soul? There will come a period when the bottom of the ocean would be deemed a refuge; when, to be crushed under falling rocks and mountains, instead of being viewed with terror as heretofore, will be earnestly desired! Yes, desired, but desired in vain! The sinner who has 'neglected so great salvation' will not be able to 'escape', nor hide himself 'from the face of him that sitteth upon the throne', nor from 'the wrath of the Lamb' (*Rev.* 6:16)!

My dear hearers! consider your condition without delay. God says to you, *Today*, if ye will hear his voice, harden not your hearts. *Today* may be the only day you have to live. Go home, enter the closet, and shut to the door; confess your sins; implore mercy through our Lord Jesus Christ. 'Kiss the Son, lest he be angry, and ye perish from the way, when his wrath is kindled but a little. Blessed are all they that put their trust in him' (*Psa.* 2:12)!